The Anxious Organization

Why Smart Companies Do Dumb Things

JEFFREY A. MILLER

Facts on Demand Press

The Anxious Organization

Why Smart Companies Do Dumb Things

Miller, Jeffrey A., 1947-
    The anxious organization : why smart companies do
  dumb things / by Jeffrey A. Miller. -- 1st ed.
    p. cm.
    ISBN: 1-889150-33-9

    1. Organizational change. 2. Industrial management.
3. Self-management (Psychology)   I. Title.

HD58.8.M55 2002   658.4'06
                           QBI02-200431

Line Art Credit: Image Club Clip Art

Cover and Interior Design: Andra Keller

Printed in Canada

Praise for
The Anxious Organization

▶

"Learning to manage your anxiety, and helping your employees manage theirs, is not a touchy-feely, 'soft skills' topic. It's a dollar and cents topic. A firm grasp of the principles in *The Anxious Organization* can mean the difference between a company that thrives and one that doesn't even survive."

Harriet Lerner, Ph.D author of *The Dance of Anger*

"Imagine that you are standing at the brink of a chasm the size of the Grand Canyon. Behind you is an organizational quagmire threatening to pull you under. What to do? Read *The Anxious Organization*. With a voice of clarity, sanity and reason Jeffrey A. Miller provides the reader with a map that says: 'here's how you can cross this chasm, and you can do it with grace and dignity and empowerment and courage.' I simply can't say enough positive things about it!"

Jean Davis, MA, Counseling Psychology
Career Transitions Specialist

"If you have a fascination with human behavior—or just a job in a workplace of stampeding wildebeests—*The Anxious Organization* is well worth your time. It explores the intricacies of organizational relationships in rich, colorful, readable prose. Great job, Jeffrey A. Miller."

Michael E. Kerr, MD
Director, the Bowen Center for the Study of the Family

CONTENTS

In Appreciation

So many people have been instrumental in bringing about *The Anxious Organization* that I am tempted to take a familiar route and begin by saying, "I don't know where to begin." This, however, would be gratuitous, since without a doubt my greatest debt is to the clients I have served, who so willingly have allowed me the honor of becoming part of their worlds and workings and from whom I've learned so much. My greatest hope is that each of you has taken as much out of our working relationship as I have.

My gratitude extends, as well, to my many teachers and role models who have patiently taken me through the challenges of learning to think about human behavior in a systems-like way. Thank you to the late Martha Urbanowski, who first urged me to add the serious study of systems to my repertoire.

Thanks, as well, to Dr. Murray Bowen, whom I never met but whose work has brought so much to all aspects of my personal and professional life.

I owe a huge debt of gratitude to the individuals who have escorted me through the sometimes discomforting but ever-satisfying journey of learning and applying Bowen Theory in my life and work. The faculty of the Center for Family Consultation has played a major role in this transforming experience. Special appreciation goes to Sydney Reed, whose wonderful teaching, supervision, and endless enthusiasm have been a true gift, and to Bob Noone, whose consultation in both the conceptual and early draft stages of *The Anxious Organization* has been of inestimable value. Thanks also to Stephanie Ferrera and Carol Moran for sharing your knowledge, thinking, experience, and research so precisely and eloquently.

To Michael Kerr, Dan Papero, and the other faculty members at the Bowen Center for the Study of the Family, thank you for your tireless efforts and excellent teaching. Your presentations and papers have contributed enormously to my learning over the years. A special note of appreciation is in order for Roberta Gilbert's review and critique of the final draft of *The Anxious Organization*.

Working on *The Anxious Organization* has allowed me at least a brief foray into the worlds of writing and publishing where I encountered the remarkably clever Catherine MacCoun, whose professional skills, talents, and ingenuity have been a *sine qua non* for the creation and execution of this book. I have also had the good fortune of working with professionals like Celia Rocks and Dottie DeHart of Rocks-DeHart Public Relations and Mark Sankey of BRB Publications, whose invaluable technical and strategic support have been infinitely appreciated.

My final expressions of gratitude go to two individuals without whom this project would never have been imaginable, much less achievable. To Jean Davis, our work together over the years has consistently shone light on vital, energizing pathways I could not have envisioned by myself. Thank you for helping to coax *The Anxious Organization* out of an anxious brain. To John Bondeson, my heartfelt thanks for your alacrity and generosity in encouraging and supporting the process of discovery that has led to the creation of this book. I especially appreciate the innumerable hours you have spent patiently listening to the rumblings and ramblings of a mind in transition.

Jeffrey A. Miller
May 1, 2002

Introduction

I admit it: *The Anxious Organization* springs from my own anxiety as a consultant. Over the years, it became evident to me that despite the essentially similar work I was doing with a number of clients, their outcomes would differ greatly. More disturbingly, there seemed to be little middle ground in the realm of results. Clients either enjoyed impressive gains in productivity from our collaboration or went away feeling they had wasted their time and money. What would explain these differences? I examined client factors such as knowledge, motivation, sheer talent, and resources, both human and fiscal. To my confusion, none of these variables correlated consistently with the success or failure of the consulting venture.

Among my clients it was not unusual to see managers of considerable skill and knowledge who brought with them impressive records of success from previous situations. Though many of these people connected well with others and developed tactics and strategies that made perfect sense to me, they didn't see much in the way of results. At the other end of the spectrum were inexperienced executives, criticized by their own people as amateurs or dilettantes. Inexplicably, many of their businesses were vibrant and growing, contributing significantly to the lives of their customers, employees, suppliers, and stockholders. Leader attributes alone could not explain why some companies did better than others. There appeared to be something intrinsically different about the organizations themselves that augured either well or poorly for success.

Various psychological and sociological theories I explored shed some light on what I was observing, but none really hit the nail on the head. Nevertheless, I sensed that I was developing a sort of internal divining rod, an ability to know quickly, when entering the world of a client, whether or not our work was destined to bear fruit. My early hunches proved remarkably accurate, even though I had no theoretical framework on which to base them. It seemed to have something to do with my own anxiety level in dealing with my client. Looking back, I discovered that the organizations that had done well were those in which I had experienced the least personal discomfort. So maybe the failures were my own fault. Maybe

I was just too darned anxious. But another compelling factor rescued me from my endless *mea culpas*. I realized I wasn't the only one who felt anxious in the organizations that weren't doing well. Most everyone else did too—from employees to suppliers to customers. Conversely, in organizations where I felt relatively at ease, so did everyone else. These less anxious organizations had some kind of leg up on the others.

It was just as this idea was beginning to gel that I first encountered Dr. Murray Bowen's Family System theory. Bowen theory, as it is often called, holds that the higher the anxiety level of an individual or group, the harder it is to think clearly, flexibly, and creatively. Fear and fantasy replace fact-based observations; decisions are made reactively rather than based on principled thinking. This sounded like what I had experienced firsthand with my two groups of clients. In the high-anxiety companies, nobody, myself included, functioned at his or her best, and the business results showed it.

Bowen theory was originally developed to explain family systems. Bowen had discovered that patients who did not engage in psychotherapy, or who were too seriously disturbed to benefit from it, could still be helped by focusing treatment on their immediate families instead. Even if just one member of the family—a parent or a sibling—changed his behavior, the dynamics of the entire family would begin to change in a way that benefited its most troubled member. Later researchers discovered that what is true of families is true of other human groups as well. Each is an emotional system in which how an individual is feeling depends to a great extent on how everyone around him or her is feeling. Over the last forty years, Bowen theory has been applied successfully by scores of consultants, clergymen, and psychotherapists. What works in families has been proven to work just as well in business, government, military, and religious communities. When I began to apply Bowen theory to my own consulting work, I was able to make headway in organizations where previously I had been stymied by my own and everyone else's anxiety level.

My purpose in writing *The Anxious Organization* is to bring Bowen theory's common-sense practical ideas to all readers, lay or professional, who wish to contribute to their own and their organizations' success. The theory's simple but sturdy framework resonates with the kinds of organizational challenges we all encounter. It guides us toward more productive workplace relationships and creative, effective deliberations and decision-making.

I hope *The Anxious Organization* will stimulate your thinking, and enable you to create the workplace experience you desire. If you wish to learn more about Bowen theory and its application, the recommended reading at the end of the book will steer you to further resources. I encourage you to contact me personally with your own workplace thinking and experiences. You can reach me at jmiller@anxiousorg.com.

Chapter 1

Primitive Guys, Inc.

Why All Organizations Are Anxious

I f you work in any organization at all, then you work in an anxious organization. How do I know this for sure? There is no other kind. All organizations are anxious organizations.

Maybe I'm starting off on the wrong foot. You probably picked up this book because you perceive a high level of anxiety in the organization for which you work and consider this a problem. You were probably expecting me to say that the anxiety you observe is a symptom of organizational dysfunction and to go on to tell you how to fix it. In a single paragraph, I have not only disappointed that expectation but also taken away any hope you might harbor of someday finding a place to work that is *not* anxious.

If you ever do find an anxiety-free workplace, my recommendation would be to start sending out resumes at once, for your employer is not going to be in business for long. Any living organism that is not anxious is on its way to being extinct. In everything that lives, anxiety is a fundamental expression of the survival instinct. It is a force of nature, as elemental as wind and rain. It is what organizations are made of and what makes them tick.

You will have a hard time seeing this if you are used to thinking of anxiety as an individual emotion, synonymous with worry or fear, and of organizations as nothing more than a collection of individuals. You will then be led to think that organizational anxiety must be nothing more or less than the sum of the individual anxieties of its members. To understand how an organization itself can be anxious, you will need to view it as a living system that is more than the sum of its parts, just as you are more than the sum of the cells your body is made of.

When a body becomes a corpse, all its parts are still there, but none of them work anymore. The death certificate may list the malfunction of a particular part as the cause of death, but what really makes a body dead is that *all* the parts have stopped. When we are alive, everything interacts with everything else. We go on being alive as long as this interaction continues. Aliveness is the active relationship of the parts, not the parts themselves.

You could say that the organization chart listing the names and functions of various members is like the corpse of a company. It doesn't tell you any more about how an organization really works than a stuffed owl tells you about a living owl. Like the body, organizations run on an incredibly complex system of interactions. They are made of the same mysterious stuff that makes our bodies alive so long as it's present and turns us into corpses the moment it disappears. In other words, an organization is a living organism.

Anxiety is the instinctive response of any living organism to a perceived threat. It is what makes you move out of the path of a speeding car, tornado, or belligerent drunk. If you didn't have anxiety, you would soon wind up dead. Likewise, a company without anxiety will soon wind up out of business.

Though humans may experience it as an emotion, organisms that we don't usually think of as emotional display anxiety too. Anxiety is simply a state of alert, of heightened readiness to respond. It is what makes cockroaches (despite what would seem to be their rather limited emotional repertoire) scurry away when the kitchen light is switched on and what makes possums play possum. In and of itself, anxiety is neither functional nor dysfunctional. It is a keen state of readiness to do something or other that may or may not be appropriate in response to a threat that may or may not be accurately perceived.

Organizing to Survive

I magine, if you will, a person living before the dawn of recorded history, free of what we have come to call civilization. Call him Joe Primitive. He is hungry for meat. The animal he must kill to get it is larger than he is. Getting meat is a risky and difficult business, and if he succeeds, his troubles are just beginning. He can't eat the whole animal in one sitting, so he hauls the leftovers into his cave. Other predators, attracted by the smell, menace him in the dark. He builds a fire to keep them away. He has to keep the fire going all night, so he doesn't get much sleep. After a few days, the meat begins to spoil. He could preserve it with salt, but that would mean leaving his cave unprotected while he went to mine the salt—which he is by now too exhausted to do. All in all, his survival system is not very efficient.

But then Joe Primitive gets a brainstorm. He realizes that other primitive guys in the vicinity are in the same predicament. If they hunted in a team, then they would have more consistent success in killing large animals. They could take turns tending the fire. With more mouths to feed, the meat would get eaten before it spoiled, and then they could go hunt more. "Why, that's the ticket!" he thinks to himself. "I'll form an organization." With the blood of his most recent kill, he drafts the world's first mission statement on the wall of his cave. He writes, "Primitive Guys, Inc. is a team-based organization dedicated to the holistic betterment of mankind as well as the profit of our shareholders through the killing of large animals and the tending of large fires."

This never happened. There was never a Joe Primitive who once tried to survive all by himself and then got the brilliant idea to form an organization. You might as well search for some ancient solitary bee that once lived outside of a hive. Survival anxiety and human affiliation arose inseparably. Survival has always been an anxious business, and forming organizations is one thing humans do and always have done about it.

When you greet your co-workers at the start of the day, you probably don't think to yourself, "I have banded together with these people for the purpose of survival." After all, the office is not some igloo where you depend on the body heat of others to keep from freezing to death. The direct deposit of your paycheck into your bank account probably does not inspire you to think that through the cooperation of your tribe, starvation has once again been averted. When physical survival is going well, we tend not to think about it much. Yet the very existence of that paycheck demonstrates that surviving is what you and your co-workers are doing together. This becomes painfully obvious only when you have reason to doubt that the paychecks will continue to arrive.

Feeling confident that we will continue to eat and not get eaten is the least common denominator of survival needs. We want to ensure not only our continued existence itself but also the *quality* of that existence. The perpetuation of ourselves as individuals is as important to most of us as the perpetuation of our species. We need the affection and fellowship of others, and we also need to feel that we are distinct from them. We can't stand the idea that we are just members of the herd. We need to feel that we are good at something, that we are making a unique contribution that we and others value. We need to feel that we are good, period. We need to feel that our lives have purpose, value, and meaning, and we want to be the ones to define that meaning. The less we worry about physical survival, the more conscious we become of these other needs. Threats to them can arouse as much anxiety as physical threats.

This is where human affiliation becomes a lot more complicated than that of, say, bees. While employed by the hive, we work for its survival, feeling any threat to it to be a threat to our own survival. Yet our personal survival is not identical to that of the hive. Though the primitive man who first decided to form an organization never actually existed, we can imagine such a person. It sounds like something we might do. We join and leave organizations at will because we are able to conceive of our individual survival as separate from that of the organization. If the hive is in trouble, we may try to save it, or we may start sending out resumes. We may even experience the survival demands of the hive as detrimental to the quality of our own individual survival. Thus, we have a dual source of anxiety. While our survival instinct moves us to join with others in order to deal more effectively with a threat, the great irony of organizational life is that those with whom we have joined can present us with new threats. We feel threatened when something threatens the hive, yet we are also capable of feeling threatened by the hive itself.

An Inventory of Anxieties

I n animals that group to survive, the group itself functions as a living organism. When there is a threat to any of its members, the whole group gets anxious. Consider what happens when a cheetah approaches a herd of wildebeests. As soon as one individual wildebeest perceives the threat, the entire herd does. For a moment the wildebeests freeze, and then suddenly, as if with one mind, the whole herd starts running away from the threat. It's as if the entire herd shares some telepathic connection that instantly transmits the anxiety of one to all the rest.

Human organizations are like wildebeest herds in this respect: the anxiety of one is transmitted to all. If one member of the group has it, then everyone has it. Human organizations differ from wildebeest herds in that members rarely agree on where the threat lies or what to do about it. As far as we know about wildebeests, all perceived threats are external to the herd. In human groups, perceived threats arise from two additional sources: threats to the entire group from within the group, and threats to the individual by the group.

In most organizations, threats to the group arising from external sources are discussed openly. If your company has a formal strategic plan, then you'll find the officially recognized threats listed there. Some typical examples include:

▶ The competition is breathing down your neck. They've introduced a better product or service, or initiated a price war.

▶ Stock performance is lackluster. Stockholders are demanding higher returns.

▶ An act of terrorism, a weather disaster (earthquake, flood, etc.), or other catastrophic public event has directly or indirectly affected your operations.

▶ Customers' demands are changing or escalating. They want it cheaper and faster than you're used to delivering it. Maybe they don't want it at all anymore.

▶ The government is getting in your way with regulatory pressures and tying you up in red tape.

▶ The government is a major customer, and they're slow to pay their bills.

▶ Raw materials and/or energy are in short supply. Prices are skyrocketing.

▶ The overall economy is in recession.

► There is a shortage of skilled workers in your industry. Recruiting qualified people is expensive and hanging on to them, even more so.

► Your industry as a whole has a negative public image (example: tobacco companies).

► You've just experienced a public-relations disaster due to an incident the company could neither have predicted nor prevented (example: the Tylenol scare).

► The company is the object of a hostile takeover bid.

You'll notice that most of these threats have a direct bearing on the economic welfare of the organization. They arouse anxiety at a very basic level of physical survival. If you and your co-workers do not cooperate to battle the threat, then the continued existence of the organization will be in jeopardy. The effect of your collective anxiety is a desire to close ranks, to work together to defeat the common enemy. That's one reason why company leaders are usually quite open about naming and discussing external threats. A common enemy tends to engender a kind of internal patriotism. Just as in a family you might fight constantly with your siblings yet rush to their defense if they are attacked by a neighborhood bully, the presence of an external threat rouses our loyalty to our organization and our determination to defend it.

The threats to an organization that arise from within it are not so often named and openly discussed by its leaders, for these tend to undermine the sense of organizational patriotism or togetherness. Members of the organization are not in open and collective agreement that these threats exist, though they may be discussed incessantly in private huddles. Some examples include:

▶ Ownership or management has recently changed, or is about to.

▶ The company has been reorganized or downsized. Employees have been laid off, and those who remain face increased workloads.

▶ The company is under-capitalized, unable to meet changing technological demands or replace obsolete equipment.

▶ Research and development efforts are lackluster. The company is slow to perceive and meet changing customer demands.

▶ Goals and objectives are not clearly and consistently articulated. Employees are not sure what they're supposed to be doing.

▶ Goals and objectives are clear but not realistic. For instance, the company is aiming for 20 per cent annual growth at a time when the economy as a whole is in recession.

▶ "Dead-wood" employees are not confronted and held accountable for performance.

▶ While preaching teamwork, the organization continues to evaluate and reward employees solely on the basis of individual performance, in effect placing them in competition with others on their team.

▶ Labor/management relations are adversarial.

▶ The organization's reputation has suffered for reasons it could and should have prevented (example: a product safety recall).

▶ Family strife in a family-owned business spills over into the workplace.

While any one of these situations undermines the economic well-being of an organization, and may even threaten its ultimate survival, internal threats seldom engender the sense of emergency that external threats do. Instead, they beget a sense of chronic, painful anxiety in which no one can seem to agree on what the threat is or what to do about it. By their very nature, internal threats tend to separate members of an organization, even to pit them against each other. Because there is not open and collective agreement about the nature of the threat, it tends not to get addressed by collective action. If you are trying to do something constructive about an internal threat, then you will likely find yourself allied with some members of the organization and in conflict with others. Someone else may even perceive *you* as the internal threat.

In addition to external and internal threats to the organization as a whole, members may experience any number of threats to themselves as individuals. The most obvious physical survival threat is the possibility of being fired or laid off. But even when we believe ourselves to be securely employed, we can experience any number of threats to the *quality* of our continued employment. Some examples include:

▶ Your survival anxieties may become focused on your own particular department or team rather than on the organization as a whole. While the company in general may be thriving, you may feel that it is not allocating sufficient resources to your own operation. Or you may be anxious that the performance of your operation is inferior to that of the rest of the company.

▶ As a boss, you are concerned about how the performance of your subordinates reflects on you. When a subordinate develops a problem, you become anxious not just about the problem itself but also about what others are thinking of you.

▶ Being a boss may conflict with your needs for affection. You become anxious over how your subordinates feel about you.

▶ You may set your sights on a promotion and view certain co-workers as rivals.

▶ Rapid changes in technology and/or the marketplace may change the nature of your work in a way that makes you feel less competent than you used to feel.

▶ A change in organizational vision or objectives may not accord well with your own vision and objectives. Your sense of meaning and purpose feels undermined.

▶ You may feel that you are being held responsible for a situation you do not have the power and/or authority to control.

▶ A reorganization may leave you feeling overworked and under-appreciated. If the company as a whole has benefited from the change, then you may feel that the benefit has come at your own expense.

While personal anxieties may not directly threaten the survival of the group, they are telegraphed to the group as quickly and powerfully as anxieties over external and internal threats to the organization as a whole. The fact that such anxieties are seldom pinpointed only makes matters worse. As a general rule, the less clearly an anxiety is articulated, the more it affects all members of a group on an unconscious, instinctual level. Recall that anxiety involves a heightened readiness to respond to threat. If you haven't a clue where the threat lies or what to do about it, then that heightened readiness is experienced as stress that you don't know how to relieve.

Anxiety Is Contagious

By now I have probably persuaded you that for organizations to be anxious is not only normal but also universal. Does that make you feel better about the anxiety in your own organization? Probably not. Not only does a high anxiety level make members very uncomfortable, but you also can probably cite instances when the anxiety in your workplace has led otherwise smart people to do dumb things.

This is how humans differ from herd animals. For wildebeests, cheetahs always represent a threat, and it is always the consensus of the herd that running away is an effective response. The collective anxiety instinct perceives accurately and responds appropriately. It's a no-brainer if you're a wildebeest because the array of possible responses is quite limited. "Run away" is the basic, one-size-fits-all solution.

Stopping to think about it would only serve to make the response less efficient.

The complexity of human civilization presents us with an indeterminate number of threats and possible solutions. Assessing the nature and degree of the threat and responding appropriately requires rational thought. This is not to say that we don't have and act on instinctive reactions to anxiety. We do. The trouble is that these instinctive reactions are often maladaptive. They can lead us to do things that distract from the real threat, or make it worse.

Consider how you came to the conclusion that you work for an anxious organization in the first place. Here are some of the behaviors you probably observed that led you to that conclusion:

▶ People taking sides with other people instead of taking stands on issues; forming clusters, coalitions, and cliques.

▶ Turf battles; people asserting their territory to the detriment of the organization as a whole; feuding and backstabbing.

▶ Blaming and scapegoating; excessive focus on the shortcomings of particular individuals or departments.

▶ Overwork. People burying themselves in tasks in order to avoid problematic interactions or hoping that increased productivity will somehow solve the problem.

▶ Conflicting instructions and mixed messages from leadership. Bold new initiatives constantly being announced and then quickly abandoned.

▶ Distancing: people not saying what they really think in meetings; lack of communication between adversaries; people literally hiding out in their offices or cubicles.

▶ Heavy turnover; people simply leaving the organization to get away from their anxiety.

These instinctive reactions to group anxiety closely mimic the behavior of other primates. They serve to contain, discharge, or displace anxiety rather than address the threat that provoked it. If you're a dominant ape, then you can make yourself feel less anxious by making another ape feel more anxious. In human groups, anxiety is moved around in a similar way. Because anxiety is experienced as an uncomfortable level of arousal (often called stress), our instinctive reaction is to get rid of it. The things we do to get rid of it almost always provoke increased anxiety in someone else. Thus, the anxiety remains in constant circulation throughout an organization while the actual threats that gave rise to it remain largely unaddressed.

This is one reason why what actually goes on in an organization often bears little resemblance to what its mission statement, organization chart, and official policies and procedures would lead you to expect. All of that represents the *rational system* of the organization—how its members think it's supposed to work when they're actually *thinking* about it. An undocumented but crucial aspect of any organization is the *emotional system* that coexists—and often competes with—the rational system. The emotional system is the complex network of reactions, interactions, and relationships that determines much of what actually occurs day to day in the workplace. If an organization is functioning differently than its rational system says it's supposed to, the emotional system is why.

Like anxiety, the emotional system is neither functional nor dysfunctional in and of itself. If there were such a thing as a company with no emotional system (there isn't), you wouldn't want to work there. You wouldn't feel any human connection to the people around you. Nor could you accomplish anything at work if you were not connected to an emotional system. The feelings you have at work give you essential social cues, facilitating many of your transactions with others. What I will be suggesting in this book is that you—and your organization—can function even more effectively if in addition to feeling, you learn to *think* about the emotional system.

According to the rational system, roles and responsibilities are clearly divided and compartmentalized. But in the emotional system, everyone is connected to everyone else. Anxiety does not respect departmental boundaries. If one person is too anxious to think clearly, then the thinking of others around that person tends to become muddled as well. This, in a nutshell, is why smart organizations do dumb things. Consider the following example.

Susan, a newly hired account manager at the Pronto advertising agency, has just been thrown the agency's most difficult client. Gwen, the client, is the publisher of a failing magazine. She believes that establishing a companion website will save the magazine, and she has hired Pronto to create and promote it. If the site does not perform up to her parent company's expectations, then Gwen will either be fired or attempt to avoid being fired by shifting the blame to the ad agency. Either way, the agency is vulnerable to losing the account. If that happens, Susan believes her own job will be in jeopardy.

When Susan is nervous, she tends to overlook details. To compensate, she takes exhaustive notes during her meetings with clients and then sends a follow-up memo recapitulating whatever agreements have been made. According to Susan's notes, the final design of the home page is to be submitted to Gwen on January 30, the date of her next quarterly sales meeting. On the morning of January 28, Gwen phones, in a fury, demanding, "Where is it?" As she remembers it, she had asked to review the design two days before the sales meeting. A flustered Susan points out that January 30 was the date listed in her post-meeting memo. Gwen, who finds Susan's constant memos tiresome and unnecessary, hadn't bothered to read it and views Susan's mentioning it now as an attempt to put her in the wrong. She thinks it should be perfectly obvious to any sensible person that she needs time to review the design before presenting it to the sales force. She accuses Susan of incompetence and slams down the phone.

Still shaking from this altercation, Susan places a frantic call to Steve, the head of the graphic-design department. Susan has been driving Steve crazy all week, calling almost hourly to demand reassurance that the January 30 deadline will be met. Steve, fed up with these constant interruptions, is working from home that day and not checking his voicemail. Unable to get through to him, Susan calls his subordinate, Cheri, and tells her she now needs the home page by the end of the day.

Cheri, likewise unable to reach Steve, feels she has no choice but to accept the new deadline and work late to meet it. As she has previously made clear to Steve, working late without advance notice is disruptive of her childcare arrangements. Though she manages to cajole her babysitter into staying two hours later, she is anxious that this still won't give her enough time to complete the job.

It would appear what we have here is an anxiety-reaction chain that follows the organizational chain of command. It proceeds from client to account manager to graphic-design manager to graphic designer and tends to confirm the old saw that "executives don't get ulcers; they give them." But that's not the end of the story. Watch what happens next.

Cheri is so worried about finishing on time that she skips both lunch and dinner. By the end of her work session, she is tired and light-headed from hunger. She finishes the home page, and it looks great. But in her fatigue, as she is uploading the page to the test server, she accidentally selects the wrong file. Originally she had presented the client with two design mock-ups—Design A and Design B. The client had chosen Design B, and that was the one Cheri went on to fully execute. The page Cheri accidentally uploads is the original mock-up of design A.

Susan would have caught the mistake before the client saw it if she had logged on first thing in the morning, as she had originally planned. But her anxiety over the previous day's altercation has kept her awake most of the night. After tossing miserably for hours, she finally takes a Valium, conks out, and oversleeps her alarm. When she arrives mid-morning at the office, she finds another urgent message from Gwen, who has already logged on to the test site and discovered the offending file. On the phone, Gwen explodes, "I told you I didn't want that design!"

Had Gwen examined the page more carefully, she would have seen immediately that it was an old mock-up rather than a completed version. But in her anxiety, she only gives it a glance. She is already predisposed to believe that the agency is going to mess up, and this is the proof.

Susan might have cleared the matter readily if she'd checked the page herself at that point. But rattled by Gwen's latest outburst, she instead heads directly for Steve's office and announces, "Cheri did the wrong page!"

Steve prides himself on his ability to keep a cool head. Normally he would calmly investigate further before concluding that Cheri had messed up. But today he is feeling guilty for having abandoned her during the previous day's crisis. He figures she probably did design the wrong page because he wasn't there to check up. So, with an air of apology, he tells Cheri that the page she'd worked on so hard the day before was the design the client had rejected. Cheri assumes this means that the client had selected Design A, not Design B. She spends the rest of the day executing Design A.

As you may be beginning to see, the anxiety in this organization is traveling in cycles, an infinite feedback loop. After being transferred down the chain of command to Cheri, it loops back to Gwen, who is made anxious by the error Cheri made in her own anxiety. After looping once more through Susan and Steve, it leads to a further error on Cheri's part, which will likely lead to a further explosion from Gwen.

Meanwhile, anxiety is also traveling in the opposite direction. Cheri, who now has to stay late for the second day in a row, is disgruntled. Steve, who was already feeling guilty, feels he is to blame for her displeasure. He resents Susan for putting him in this position.

To escape the bad vibes coming from Cheri, Steve heads for the employee lounge where he finds Rocky, his counterpart in the copy department. "Susan is driving me nuts!" he bursts out. Rocky is sympathetic. The copywriters have been having similar troubles with Susan. In the coming days, their mutual displeasure with Susan becomes the theme of every conversation between Steve and Rocky. Together they conclude that she's a nitwit and not going to last long with the agency.

Before long, Susan begins to notice that all of the creative staff are giving priority to the projects of other account managers and failing to return her calls. Her sense of impending doom intensifies. She sleeps poorly. Her concentration, which was never great to begin with, diminishes further. She bungles additional details, leading Gwen to be more than ever convinced that she's incompetent. But changing agencies at this point would cost a fortune and delay the debut of the website—a fiasco that would cost Gwen her own job. So all Gwen can think to do is to go on calling up and yelling.

Who is causing the problem? You might be tempted to say that it is Gwen because our story begins with her first outburst. But if you were to ask Gwen, she would say that she was already worried prior to the deadline incident because Susan didn't appear "with it," was so busy taking notes during meetings that she didn't listen well. If you were to ask Susan why she acts like that in meetings, she would say that she is afraid this client is setting her up to be scapegoated, and she needs a "paper trail" to prove that the orders she followed were the orders the client gave. What she is doing to protect herself from the client's displeasure turns out to be the very thing that most displeases the client.

Why are Susan and Gwen so afraid of being fired in the first place? To understand that, we would need to consider other players. The CEO of Susan's agency, when he assigned her Gwen's account, quipped that it would be her "trial by fire." He meant this remark to put her at ease. He meant to say, "We all know this client is a pain." Susan mistook him to mean that the account was a probationary ordeal, the outcome of which would determine her fate in the company. As Susan in her anxiety gradually lost the respect of both the client and the creative staff, her worst fear eventually came true.

The CEO's actual meaning—"this client is a pain"—is an expression of his own anxiety. He is afraid that the agency will lose her account and is setting up her difficult personal characteristics as an alibi. When Gwen shows up at the agency for a meeting, her reputation precedes her. On an instinctive level, she can feel that she is being placated like some dangerous animal, and she instinctively responds as if she were indeed a dangerous animal. Being discombobulated by their fear, the staff of the agency doesn't serve her well, which makes her afraid that they will blow the project. The more afraid she feels, the more aggressively she behaves, which discombobulates them even more and leads to even poorer service.

Steve would, at first glance, appear to be too level headed to be an anxiety carrier. He prides himself on not flying off the handle or dumping on his own staff. But his method of managing his anxiety—leaving the office when it begins to stress him out—ends up distributing anxiety to both his subordinates and the account managers who can't reach him when they need him. His informal huddles with the copywriters also have the effect of exacerbating Susan's growing scapegoat status.

The more closely you examine the situation, the harder it is to lay blame. The anxiety and the maladaptive responses to it have no clear point of origin. Instead of linear cause and effect, you have a complex and ever-widening system of vicious circles. What each person is doing to relieve his or her own anxiety has the effect of shifting anxiety to someone else.

To see situations in this organic, systemic way is the beginning of genuine insight into what's really going on in anxious organizations and what you might potentially do about it. While the bad news is that anxiety is highly contagious and tends to be self-perpetuating, the good news it that any member of the organization can change the system by changing his or her own behavior.

Skeptical? You're not alone. Each of the players in our ad-agency scenario would likewise be skeptical, for each one feels that how he or she is acting is being caused by how someone else is acting. Each is coping to the best of his or her ability as an individual. When trying to cope individually, we tend to see ourselves as the isolated effect of an isolated cause. We focus on our own anxiety and what we might do to relieve it without recognizing its source in the anxiety of others and our own coping mechanisms as contributors to their anxiety. It is only when we can step back and view the entire system that we get a handle on how to influence it in a saner and more productive direction.

In Summary ...

 An organization is more than the sum of the individuals who belong to it. It is a living system of relationships in which everyone is connected to everyone else.

 Anxiety is an instinctive response to a real or perceived threat to survival. In animals this instinct leads reliably to an effective response to the threat. Because the threats faced by human organizations are more varied and subtle, it takes rational thought to determine the most effective response. People tend not to think well when they are overly anxious. Their automatic responses to threat are, therefore, quite often counterproductive.

 Organizational anxiety arises from three main sources: external threats, internal threats, and the miscellaneous anxieties of its individual members. Regardless of the source of the threat, anxiety is felt collectively. If one member is anxious, then everyone gets anxious.

 In seeking to relieve their own anxiety, individuals usually pass it on to someone else. Thus, anxiety tends to travel in cycles that have no clear starting point while the underlying cause of the anxiety goes unaddressed.

Because an organization is a system in which all members are connected, an individual can change the entire system by changing his or her own behavior.

Chapter 2

This Is Your Brain on Stress

How anxiety leads to doing dumb things

The premise of this book is that you can change an anxious organization for the better if you are able to think clearly about it. One of the ironies of this book is that thinking clearly is the very thing we find hardest to do when in an anxiety-provoking situation.

The physical effects of anxiety are familiar and, more often than not, we find them unpleasant. Our bodies are telling us to DO SOMETHING and, until we do, our bodies remain in a state of agitation. Unfortunately, what our bodies are telling us to do is quite often the *wrong* thing.

The body's response to anxiety is controlled by the most primitive part of our brain, the part it has in common with those of lower animals and reptiles. It is designed to respond appropriately to physical threats, and it is very good at this. The three things it knows to do about danger are to fight, run away, or freeze. It instantly determines which of these responses to implement and prepares the body accordingly. From the point of view of the "lizard brain," thinking about what to do is neither necessary nor desirable. Thinking would only complicate matters and slow the body down.

The middle portion of our brain, which we have in common with other mammals, mediates our emotions. When the reptile brain is sending out fight signals, your mid-brain is saying to you, "I'm angry!" It translates flight signals as "Get me out of here!" If the reptile brain is telling your body to freeze, then you experience yourself as stunned. Being more sophisticated than the reptile brain, the mid-brain is capable of a lot of emotional nuances. The fight signal may be interpreted as anything from mild sarcasm to a desire to rip out your adversary's aorta with your teeth.

The highest part of our brains, the cerebral cortex, is capable of performing the complex calculations that inform you that ripping out your boss's aorta with your teeth is probably not a prudent career move. Since most of the threats we humans encounter are not physical, the higher brain spends a lot of time overruling the simplistic physical solutions proposed by the lizard brain. Alas, by the time these vetoes have been issued, the lizard brain has already set in motion the physiological changes that prepare us to fight, flee, or play dead. Energy courses through our bodies that we don't know what to do with. We feel "wired" because we *are* wired—physiologically wired to do what our thinking tells us we'd better not do.

In order to think about what to do instead, we need to subdue the hormonal suggestions our stress responses are making to our central nervous system. In layman's terms, this is called "calming down." The literature on stress reduction is full of recommendations about how to do it. You are probably already trying to follow some of these recommendations. Let me explain why it isn't working.

Much of what we try to do to relieve stress is simply a displacement of the fight/flight/freeze response. You've decided not to hit your customer, so you go hit an inanimate object, such as a punching bag or a golf ball. If it is impractical to run away, then you run laps around the block. Or else you *get* away. You go on vacation, take a "mental health day" or a coffee break, or escape mentally into fantasy or entertainment. Or perhaps you meditate, a spiritually advanced version of the "hold real still and maybe they'll think you're dead" response. As an alternative to displacing your physiological response, you may try to overwhelm it with a competing physiological response, such as the effects of beer, St. John's Wort, or Fettuccine Alfredo.

Frequent and/or prolonged anxiety reactions wear out the body. For the sake of your health, you need to dispel the physical effects of anxiety, and any of the commonly recommended methods of stress release will do that. Exercise, meditation, breaks, hobbies, social support, and so forth are all helpful in reducing your vulnerability to stress-related illness. But none of these methods reduce stress *per se*. Your body has become agitated in the first place for a reason. It wants to respond to a perceived threat. In displacing or dispelling your physiological stress reaction, you have not succeeded in eliminating the threat. If it's real—or if you continue to perceive it as real—it will keep causing you anxiety until it is addressed.

Consider what happens when you try to relieve stress by going on a two-week vacation. You spend the fortnight prior to your departure frantically preparing for whatever is likely to ensue in the workplace during your absence and a fortnight afterwards trying to clean up whatever it is that *has* ensued. Two weeks of getting away from it all cost you four weeks of intensified "it all."

The real point of calming down is that we think better when we're calm. If you quiet your body's stress response and don't use the inner peace and quiet you've achieved to think, then the original threat is likely to return with a vengeance and with it, your stress response. If you don't have a new thought after applying your stress-reduction technique of choice, then that technique may actually become part of the problem. Steve's strategy of working from home and ignoring his voicemail took its toll in doubled stress the next day. Susan's strategy of taking a Valium provided her with needed rest but set her up to function poorly the following morning. Neither Susan nor Steve succeeded in addressing the actual source of their anxiety.

Don't get me wrong. Calming down is important, even essential. But it is simply a prelude to the real work of anxiety reduction, which is thinking. One trick is to distance yourself from the situation as long—and *only* as long—as it takes to quiet down the propaganda blaring from your lizard brain. With some practice you can learn to do that while in the midst of an anxious situation.

Take a Six-Second Vacation

We need to get some emotional distance from a situation that is making us anxious before we can think clearly about it. A vacation or a good night's sleep can work wonders in refreshing our perspective. But what if you can't get away? What if you're in the middle of a meeting, conversation, or other incident that is triggering your anxiety and you need to be able to think clearly about it right now?

Try taking a six-second vacation. It works like this:

- Inhale for two seconds, sending the air where you need a little help. It can be sent to any part of your body, mind, or spirit, or you can direct it to a troubling idea, a present worry, a concern, or even a recurring theme.
- Exhale for two seconds, releasing all muscle tension in your body, starting at the head and moving to the toes. Think of yourself as a boneless chicken.
- Do NOTHING for two seconds.

The Thinking That Works— and the Thinking That Doesn't

A t this point, maybe you want to protest that you are already thinking about the source of your anxiety. You think about it constantly. You think about it at 3 a.m. You think about it even while jogging or watching a movie or knocking back a few beers or whatever else you do when you're trying not to think about it.

The kind of thinking that works is not the kind of thinking most people are doing when they are thinking about their anxiety. That's often because they're not really thinking *about* their anxiety at all. They are thinking the thoughts that anxiety has proposed. Susan, for example, is thinking, "What if I get fired?" and, "How can I keep Gwen from blaming me?" and, "It's her own fault for not reading my memo," and "How can I get Steve back on my side?" and "How could Cheri have been so careless?" The one thing Susan is not thinking is, "I am anxious."

But, you may wish to argue, that goes without saying. Obviously Susan is anxious and obviously she knows it. That's why she took a Valium. Nevertheless, Susan's anxiety itself has not become the specific object of her contemplation. If she were to think about her anxiety in and of itself, she would be able to see that it is not merely an effect of the outward situation but also one of the factors that is creating that situation. She would see that it was anxiety that led her to bury the client in memos, anxiety that led her to pester Steve to the point where he started ducking her calls, and anxiety that led her to jump to the conclusion that Cheri had designed the wrong page. If her anxiety itself were to become the subject of her ruminations, then she would be able to think, "As a result of anxiety, I'm doing things that make the situation worse."

This is hard to see, for when we are acting out of anxiety, we usually feel that we are doing the most natural thing in the world, what anyone else in our place would do, the only thing to do that makes sense under the circumstances. That is the essence of the problem. Our response has become inflexible. We don't see other options. Not only that, but our automatic responses tend to provide temporary relief from the symptoms of anxiety. We don't notice that our behavior is anxiety-driven because our habitual coping mechanisms are making us feel better at the very moment when we are doing something that, over the long run, is going to make matters worse.

Steve was doing the most natural thing in the world when he "vented" to Rocky in the employee lounge. A lot of stress experts will tell you that venting or "seeking social support" are healthy ways of coping with anxiety. That is absolutely true in the same sense it is true that if you are giving ulcers, then you probably aren't getting them. If we are looking at Steve in isolation, thinking only about how to relieve his personal stress, complaining to a co-worker is a pretty good way to go about it. Rocky, too, may have felt better, since he had some of the same complaints. Their conversations validate what each is feeling, reassure them that "it's not just me." At the same time, this mutual validation serves to solidify their negative feelings about Susan. After several such conversations, the idea of Susan's incompetence has become a monument, an institution. They feel justified in withdrawing their cooperation from her, which leads to more anxiety on her part and further anxiety-driven demonstrations of her alleged incompetence. While these demonstrations may give them the dubious satisfaction of saying, "I told you so," they will also cause a lot of wear and tear on Steve, Rocky, and their staffs.

Am I saying that Steve shouldn't have confided his frustration to Rocky? Not really. As a temporary coping mechanism, it got the job done. He discharged his anger. He and Rocky had a good laugh at Susan's expense, and he returned to his office in a better mood than when he'd left it. Feeling temporarily better is an opportunity to think better. That is the opportunity that Steve missed when he gave no further thought to his own anxiety.

What might he have thought if he did think about it? He would have discovered that, despite the pride he takes in being calm, some of his actions are driven by anxiety and transfer anxiety to those around him. The risk—and also the potential reward—in such reflections is the discovery that he is not the hapless victim he feels himself to be as a middle manager. He is an active member of the system that is bugging him and, as such, has the power to influence it.

If he were here, Steve would protest that he is already trying to influence it. He has given a great deal of thought to how to cope with Susan's annoying behavior. He asked himself outright, "How can I get Susan to stop pestering me constantly for reassurance?" and "How can I get her to stop creating eleventh-hour emergencies for my staff?" The best solution he could think of was to stop returning her calls. He reasoned that if he were unavailable as a dumping ground for Susan's anxiety, then she'd have to figure out something else to do with it.

Susan, too, believes that she is coming up with rational solutions. She has asked, "How can I keep the client from arbitrarily changing her demands and then blaming me when they aren't met?" and concluded that the best solution is to put everything in writing. She has asked, "How can I make sure that the creative staff will meet their deadlines?" and concluded that reminding them of the deadline six times a day is a good way to go about it.

Both Steve and Susan are thinking about problems and trying to come up with rational solutions. The trouble is that they are thinking about the *wrong* problem. The problem, as they define it, is someone else's behavior, and the solution involves attempting to control that behavior.

This doesn't work. It can't work. What other people think, feel, and do is beyond our control. If our solution to our anxiety involves getting someone else to change, then it is doomed to failure. There is no way Susan can keep Gwen from blaming her if that is what Gwen feels like doing. There is no way Steve can prevent Susan's calling to seek reassurance when she is worried or stop her from making frantic requests at the last minute.

In his focus on changing Susan, Steve has neglected to ask himself the one question that is his, and his alone, to answer. Is it reasonable to ask his staff to stay late to meet a sudden change in assignment or deadline? Is this something he is willing to do? This is his decision to make as manager of the design department, and he has so far avoided making it. He has allowed events to make the decision for him.

It's a difficult question. Whatever position he takes will have its downside. Though Susan is the worst offender, she is not the only account executive in the agency that makes last-minute demands. The belief of the CEO and of all the account execs is that the agency will lose business if they don't give customers exactly what they want when they want it. They have come to pride themselves on considering no client demand too unreasonable. If a client asks them to produce an eight-page brochure on a week's notice, then the agency somehow manages to come through. This naturally leads clients to conclude that a week's notice must be sufficient. In a sense, the agency has trained its customers to expect breakneck responsiveness, and now everyone is anxious that they will lose customers if they don't continue to deliver.

At the same time, Steve's success as a manager depends on his being able to attract and hold on to talented designers, and he believes one way to do that is to be sensitive to their needs for work/life balance. When he interviewed Cheri, she told him that, due to her childcare arrangements, she would have a problem staying late without advance notice. He said, "I understand." Cheri construed his "I understand" to mean that he would honor her needs, and this was a factor in her choosing to come to work for the agency. If last-minute assignments continue to disrupt her personal life, then she may change her mind. Her quitting would leave his department short staffed, further compromising its ability to meet the demands of clients.

So as Steve sees it, there is nothing he can do. What he means by this is that there is nothing he can do *without incurring someone's displeasure*. The question in his mind has subtly shifted from "What is the reasonable thing to do?" to "What can I do without making someone mad?" In effect, the question has become, "How can I control the reactions of the account executives and my staff?" It is an unanswerable question because he *can't* control how they will react.

Planting Your Feet (Instead of Jerking Your Knees)

M aybe you are expecting me to break in here with a painless solution. That's what clients are usually hoping for when they call in a consultant. They hope I will show them some completely painless option that they've somehow overlooked. When that happens, I become the bearer of bad news: there are no painless solutions.

It may be of some consolation in this case to point out that *not* deciding has not been painless either. The net result of avoiding the issue is that now both Susan and Cheri are unhappy. Cheri's personal life did get disrupted, and Susan didn't get the web page she needed at the time she needed it. Cheri no longer trusts that Steve will support her scheduling requirements, and Susan no longer trusts that his department will come through in a pinch. In not taking a stand, he has managed to avoid being directly blamed by either of them, but the underlying distrust he has incurred will likely lead to further anxiety-driven behavior from both.

No matter what Steve does—or doesn't do—he's going to disappoint someone. Realizing this, he can free his attention from the unproductive question of "How can I control the reactions of other people?" and turn it back to the original and highly productive question of "What is the *reasonable* thing for me to do in this situation?" His options are either to inform employees that they will indeed be asked to stay late on occasion without advance notice or to inform account execs that last-minute requests may not always be accommodated. It is Steve's job as department head to weigh the consequences of each choice to the system as a whole, make a judgment call, and communicate it forthrightly to all concerned. This is called "taking an I-position."

To take an I-position is to identify and state to others what you know, believe, and/or intend to do. It is based on your best thinking about the problem at hand. It is about facts and issues rather than feelings and personalities. An I-position states what you believe to be true and valid regardless of the emotional pressures of the situation.

This leads to another of the great ironies of this book. Anxiety is systemic. To understand what is making you anxious at work, you have to look at the entire emotional system, see that what is going on with you is inextricably related to what is going on with everyone around you. Yet to influence that system in a less anxious direction, what you will need to do is to differentiate yourself from it. That means calling a halt to your automatic, anxiety-driven reactions and coming up with something to do that is neither automatic nor anxiety driven. It means identifying the question that is yours to answer, deciding what you think, and letting others know what you have decided.

As Steve was soon to discover, deciding what you think can be surprisingly difficult. The first "thoughts" he shared with me about the issue were actually emotional responses.

"Okay, here's how I see it," he began. "The whole deadline crisis was really Susan's fault. She didn't communicate clearly with the client. Cheri was an innocent victim. So I think the fair thing to do would be to side with Cheri next time this happens."

Don't be misled by his judicious tone here. This is emotion talking. Between the lines he is saying that he is angry with Susan and feels guilty in relation to Cheri. Now he's preparing to don his Superman tights and champion the underdog.

"Steve, it sounds like you're deciding this thing on the basis of personalities," I point out.

He shakes his head vehemently. "Not at all. It's the principle of the thing."

"The principle being...?"

"Cheri shouldn't have to suffer for Susan's mistakes."

"Okay. But what if Susan hadn't made a mistake? What if she had what you would consider a very good reason to move up the deadline?"

"I don't know. I guess what I'm saying wouldn't really apply to a situation like that."

"In other words, if you don't know who to blame, then you don't know what position to take. What you call 'the principle of the thing' is that wrongdoers should be punished."

"I wouldn't have put it exactly like that but...."

"But?"

"But, yeah, I guess that's what I mean. Besides, if I have to have one of them angry with me, I'd rather it was Susan. I don't think she's going to last long in this place. And I want to keep Cheri around. She's a great designer and a gem to work with. Not a whiner. That's the thing, you see. She's very accommodating, always willing to go the extra mile. It's easy to take advantage of a person like that. Someone has to draw the line."

"Someone such as you."

"Well, yeah."

"What if I told you that it was Cheri's line to draw? Instead of taking your own I-position, you're trying to take Cheri's."

Steve considers this for a moment. "Okay, I see your point. But I don't want her to draw the line by quitting. It would be a real hassle to lose her."

"So, speaking as the head of the design department, trying to prevent employee turnover is one of your considerations."

"Precisely."

"Do you see how that's different from wanting to protect Cheri?"

Steve looks puzzled. "It's more abstract. Is that what you mean?"

"You're talking now about the real needs of your organization, not personalities and feelings."

"Yeah. I need Susan to stop driving us all nuts!" he retorts.

"Let's try taking Susan out of the picture for a moment. As I understand it, other account executives also make last-minute demands on occasion. Is that right?"

"Sure. They all do, once in a while. Not as often as Susan. And somehow with the others it's not as annoying."

"How so?"

"It's that whiny voice of hers. The minute I hear her say, 'Ste-eee-ve,' I know I'm in for it. Look, I don't mean to sound chauvinistic, but if there's one thing I can't stand, it's a hysterical female."

"Sounds like you speak from experience."

"Yeah, lifelong experience. My mom....Well, never mind. No reason to drag her into this."

"Would you say that Susan and your mother are alike in certain respects?"

"She didn't start out that way. My mom didn't. But when my dad left, she fell to pieces. Couldn't seem to handle any of life's little ups and downs anymore. It was always, "Ste-eee-ve, the garbage disposal is clogged," or, "Ste-eee-ve, how am going to pay the telephone bill?" I was the oldest, so suddenly all of this stuff was supposed to be my problem to solve."

"How did you handle that?"

"Not very well, I suppose. I hid out in my room with the headphones on a lot." A dawning thought breaks across Steve's face. "Kind of like what I do with Susan, come to think of it."

"How'd it work? Hiding out in your room."

"Just made her more hysterical. In the end, I'd always give in and bail her out. Gee, this is starting to feel like therapy. Are you telling me I need to work through my childhood stuff with my mother before I can solve my problem with Susan?"

"Not at all. The relevance of childhood stuff is simply that when a situation makes us anxious, we tend to flash back to similar anxious situations in the past and react in whatever way we learned to react as kids. If you're doing what comes naturally, then it usually means you're doing what you've done many times before. For you, what comes naturally is to first attempt to hide out and then to relent and come to the rescue."

"Which didn't really work then and doesn't work now. Yeah, I see that. So you're saying that instead of having this knee-jerk response, I should...well, I don't know. I haven't the foggiest idea what to do instead."

"*Now* you're thinking."

"I am?" Steve grins ruefully. "I feel pretty stupid, to tell you the truth."

"What you were doing before that you called 'thinking' was actually reacting—to personalities, emotions, past situations. Once you see that, you've cleared the deck. You can begin to consider the dynamics of the current situation in a more objective way. So let's take it once more from the top. The question at hand is whether you are willing to ask employees to stay late on short notice to fulfill last-minute requests from account executives."

"You mean employees and account executives in the abstract, right? Not just Susan and Cheri."

"Precisely. What are your thoughts on the issue?"

"Well, to go back to your earlier question, I see now that it really doesn't matter whether the last-minute request is the account executive's fault or not. Either way, my staff is inconvenienced. But that's par for the course in advertising."

"Do you mean then that having to stay late is a condition of employment that designers must be prepared to accept if they want to work in your agency?"

Steve falls silent for a long time. "I'm not sure," he says finally. "I never really thought about that one before. It's kind of a complicated question. Can I get back to you on it?"

This response is typical and a good sign. When we're reacting out of anxiety, answers tend to come quickly. Reliable, principle-based thinking takes more time.

When we meet again the following week, Steve announces that he still hasn't come to a decision. Nevertheless, he is energetic and eager to share his many new observations on the subject. "Where I'm stuck, you see, is that it seems like either decision I make will lead to the same negative outcome. If I don't accept last-minute requests from the account execs, then we may occasionally let down a client and maybe lose an account. But if I keep letting them drive my staff haywire, then I may lose good people. That's actually happened in the past. We still end up letting down the client because we're short staffed or because my people are so stressed out that they start making mistakes, like what happened with Cheri. It seems to me the real problem is that the account execs make unrealistic promises to clients so that disappointing them sometimes becomes inevitable. But, as you say, what the account execs do is not really under my control."

He pauses as a new thought occurs to him. "I've been trying to decide this on the basis of what best serves the clients, but since that seems to be a wash, maybe I should decide it on some other basis."

"Such as…?"

"I don't know. Maybe this is being emotional again, but when I ask an employee to stay late at the last minute, I never feel right about it. I know you'll say it's the employee's decision whether he or she wants to put up with that, but I really feel employees shouldn't have to. I want this agency to value my staff because of the quality of their work, not because they're doormats. Frankly, I think our clients would value us more if we didn't placate them all the time. It's like the whole agency is coming from a position of weakness. That bothers me."

"And you feel that you, yourself, are sometimes coming from a position of weakness? Does that happen?"

"Yeah. You see, that's what I really hate. When I beg an employee to stay late, I feel really lame."

"Why is that?"

"Because a department head is supposed to manage things so that employees can predict their workload from day to day. When I make chaos of their personal lives, I feel like I'm a lousy manager. I'm capable of handling things better than that, and I believe I ought to. Maybe you'll say that's an unrealistic expectation to have in a place like this, but it's what I really think. It's the kind of manager I want to be," he concludes firmly.

"It sounds like you've discovered your I-position," I observe.

"Yeah. I guess I have. Yikes."

Notice that the decision Steve has come to after all this reflection is the same one he proposed at the beginning of our first conversation. What has changed are his reasons. Initially he was being motivated by his anger with Susan, his impulse to rescue Cheri, and habitual reactions to "hysterical females" that date back to his adolescence. Once he recognized and acknowledged these feelings, he was able to set them aside and consider the matter more objectively. It was then that the true "principle of the thing" became clear to him. He was able to define what he believed his own responsibilities to be and the course of action that would best fulfill them.

Another department head might have come to a different conclusion, deciding, for example, that his responsibility was to put the needs of the account executives first. That conclusion would be just as defensible. An I-position need not be "right" in any absolute and universal sense. What matters is identifying the stand that best expresses one's own convictions. When you take an I-position, you are telling others in your organization something about who you are. You are giving them a realistic idea of what they can expect from you.

But hasn't Steve been expressing who he is all along? His irritation with Susan, his concern for Cheri, his desire to distance himself from the situation, and the comfort he took in venting to Rocky were all genuine feelings. We tend to feel most like our true selves when having emotional reactions that are at once strong and familiar. "Whiners really annoy me," Steve might say. "That's just who I am." Yet on closer examination, these strong and familiar reactions were being provoked by factors external to Steve: what people around him were doing in the present and what his mother had done in the past. His reactions arose so automatically that he didn't experience himself as having a choice about them.

Nothing external to Steve provoked him to conclude that it is the role of a department head to exercise foresight in managing the workload of his employees. That is what he really thinks when he is able to detach himself momentarily from external pressures. It is who Steve really is when he's not being jerked around by the systemic anxiety in his workplace. In other words, in order to know and express his "real self," Steve needed to stop reacting automatically and *think*. We discover our true selves when we make calm, clear, and conscious choices.

Pocketing the Hot Potato

Did you ever play the game of Hot Potato when you were a kid? The object of the game is to throw the hot potato to someone else as soon as you catch it. That's how anxiety moves through an organization: as soon as one person catches it, he or she throws it to someone else. When you engage in principled thinking, it's as if you've caught the potato and, instead of passing it on, slipped it into your pocket and allowed it to cool off. Instead of having to catch the hot potato, the next person in the anxiety cycle has an opportunity to think calmly. Anything you yourself do that is not anxiety driven can have a remarkably calming effect on the whole system.

What I've just said is true overall, and in the long run. But if it were as simple as that, this book wouldn't have another six chapters. If taking an I-position were as easy as I've made it sound so far, then everyone would be doing it already. The sober truth of the matter is that when people are used to playing Hot Potato and you pocket the potato, their immediate reaction is often to go look for another one. Meanwhile, the one you've already got in your pocket may be giving off quite a lot of heat.

When we are trying to meet the conflicting demands a system is placing on us, the instinct to avoid conflict often leads us to avoid taking any position at all. By not saying a clear Yes or No, we may feel that we are pleasing everyone, or at least avoiding their displeasure. We manage to evade the acute anxiety of open conflict only to place ourselves in the chronic anxiety of a no-win situation. Taking an I-position is following the opposite course. You liberate yourself from chronic anxiety by facing up to a situation that may cause you acute anxiety, at least for a time. You may well find that your anxiety, and that of others around you, gets worse before it gets better.

Organizations are into self-preservation. It is the instinct of every system. Because it is an instinct and not a rational thought, it's not always smart. It may even work against the organization's long-term survival. Nevertheless, the instinct is very strong and kicks in the moment any individual in the system disrupts the status quo by doing something new. Take a stick and stir it around in an anthill, and immediately the ants set to work trying to restore it to its original condition. They do not stop to consider that your action is actually a rather interesting design statement. Organizations are like anthills in that respect. Change anything—even for the better—and the first response of everyone around you will be to scramble to restore the system to its original condition.

When Steve finally identified his I-position, his first response was "Yikes!" He can already see that his position is going to be resisted by some of his co-workers and that the ensuing conflicts may cause him some heightened anxiety. Yet his new perspective energizes him. He feels less guilty in relation to Cheri, seeing that she has her own choices to make and that he is not ultimately responsible for her job satisfaction. He also feels less angry with Susan, realizing that she has been riding roughshod over his needs because he himself has never clearly stated them. He sees how coming from a position of strength might even inspire others in the agency to do the same, how the whole place might eventually become less frantic. Nevertheless, his story will have several more installments before we arrive at a happy ending. For now, let's leave him in his moment of shaky triumph at having differentiated himself from the system long enough to discover what he really thinks.

In Summary...

 When we feel threatened, our bodies prepare to respond to the threat by fighting, running away, or playing dead. Since these are seldom appropriate responses to threats arising in the workplace, our bodies are constantly preparing to do what our minds have no intention of doing. This physiological arousal for which we have no use is called stress.

 Many stress-reduction techniques are effective at relieving the effects of physical overexcitement and are good for your overall health. But reducing the symptoms of anxiety does not get rid of its underlying triggers. For that, you need to think.

 The solutions we come up with when anxious often have the effect of making the objective situation worse by transferring anxiety to someone else. In order to come up with better solutions, it is necessary first to recognize that you are anxious and calm down.

 Basing what we do on how we imagine other people are going to react is anxiety-driven behavior. When we feel we are in a no-win situation, it is usually because we believe we have to please everyone, which is rarely possible. We cannot control the reactions of other people and attempting to do so only raises our own anxiety, as well as theirs.

 Sound problem solving arises from thinking about issues and principles rather than feelings and personalities. A principle-based stance is called an I-position.

 Taking an I-position may temporarily raise chronic anxiety to an acute level as underlying issues and conflicts become more clearly delineated. In the long run, however, when one person takes an I-position, the entire system is able to calm down.

Chapter 3

You Are Not a Wildebeest

The Herd Instinct and Its Discontents

Readers who have so far observed Gwen from the point of view of the Pronto Agency, where she does not appear at her best, may be amused to learn that she is the publisher of *Team Player Today*. Founded in the 1930s, this magazine for clerical workers was originally called *Working Gal*. Later incarnations of the same publication were called *Modern Secretary* and *Today's Administrative Assistant*. Its most recent title reflects both the trend toward a less hierarchical management style and Gwen's own passion for sports metaphors.

Gwen is also a great believer in staff teambuilding retreats. One year she engaged a facilitator who, after administering a personality test, classified each staff member according to what type of circus performer he or she was most like. There were tightrope walkers, lion tamers, knife throwers, sideshow barkers, clowns, and ringmasters. This exercise gave the staff a safe way to air their conflicts and differences. "No wonder we're clashing," you'll still hear one say to another. "As a tightrope walker, I need to give you more slack." Or, "As a lion tamer, I'm always forgetting that clowns don't respond well to the whip." Everyone came out of the retreat feeling that they understood each other a great deal better.

The following year, the staff spent a day at a paintball camp. They still boast of their victory over the staff of *Hot Competition* and wear their paint-spattered "Team *Team Player*" tee shirts on casual Fridays. Yet, despite their evident *esprit de corps*, Team *Team Player* has not, in recent years, succeeded in turning a profit.

If you ask Maggie, the editorial director, to diagnose the problem, she'll get up first to close her office door and then whisper, "It's those guys in sales. They keep cutting ad-space prices and then boast that ad sales are up by 30 percent. Sure, space devoted to ads is up by 30 percent, but revenue is flat. And that means 30 percent less space for editorial content. We're giving less value to our subscribers. But there I go talking like a knife thrower again," she adds sheepishly. "And I do see what they're up against. The clerical profession is dwindling. We're serving a vanishing market."

Tom, the ad sales director, sees it differently. "As renewals have declined, there's more pressure on us to sell space to make up the difference. At the same time, we have to keep cutting rates because the circulation numbers aren't there. We're working our tails off while those clowns over in circulation sit around with their feet up their desks all day. But, hey, you could expect me to say that. I'm a lion tamer. Anyway, I wouldn't want to be in their shoes. No matter how often you update the name, we're still publishing the same old *Working Gal*."

Gerard, in circulation, just throws up his hands. "Look, we're supposed to be selling this thing to secretaries. *What* secretaries?"

About a month before she made her first appearance in these pages, Gwen emerged shaken from a meeting with the director of her parent company. "I have a special affection for our *Working Gal*," he began, glancing mistily at the faded cover of the inaugural issue hanging across from his desk. A smartly hatted, white-gloved secretary smiled perkily back at him from within her mahogany frame. "It was Granddad's flagship publication when he founded this firm back in 1932. But, Gwen, it's killing us. *Hot Competition* has doubled its subscriber base over each of the past three years while our old gal is in free fall. We're going to have to pull the plug."

Gwen's stomach knotted at the prospect of dismantling her beloved team. Perhaps positions could be found for most of them on other publications of the parent company, but they would no longer be Team *Team Player*. They were like family to her and to each other. She was not about to let her family be torn apart without a fight. Jutting her jaw out fiercely, she said, "Look, we're not going to shy at the final hurdle. Just give me two more quarters. I promise you, I can hit this thing out of the ballpark." Behind her head, the smartly hatted, white-gloved secretary seemed to look at the director imploringly. With some misgivings, he granted her a six-month stay of execution.

On the next casual Friday, Gwen called her staff into her office, where two extra-large stuffed pizzas, purchased out of her own pocket, awaited them on the conference table. Forthrightly, she presented them with the problem and then announced the solution that had come to her during one of several sleepless nights. "It's time for us to enter the new millennium," she began. Her staff looked back with interest. They had been thinking the same thing.

"Our readers are all on the web, and that's where we need to be." Gwen continued. "We have three months to launch *Team Player Today, the e-zine.* I know that's a really tight timeframe, but we're a really tight team. I'm expecting each and every one of you to step up to the plate and kick this one through the goal posts. Now tell me frankly what obstacles you see," she added democratically. "It's important that we all communicate honestly about this."

Gerard chose that moment to help himself to a fourth slice of stuffed pizza. Maggie, the editor, was wishing that Gwen would stop mixing metaphors. "There I go, knife throwing again," she thought to herself. She went back to picking bits of anchovy, onion, and olive out of her pizza slice and arraying them in neat piles on the side of her paper plate. Tom leapt into the breach to say that he didn't see any problem with selling web banner ads to current advertisers, provided he could offer them a generous introductory discount. At this, Gwen beamed her approval.

Gerard chewed hastily, then put in, "If we offered some password-protected features for subscribers only, then that becomes an extra incentive to subscribe to the magazine. Package deal, in other words. Think you guys in editorial could come up with something like that, Maggie?"

Maggie looked up from her denuded slice of pizza long enough to smile wanly. "Oh sure. No problem."

As the group continued to discuss the particulars of their new project, Gwen looked on with growing satisfaction. All those team-building retreats had really paid off, she reflected. Team *Team Player* was rising to the occasion admirably. They would all pull together to meet this crisis. They would leave *Hot Competition* in the dust.

Smart Members, Dumb Group

What's wrong with this picture? Having eavesdropped on the private thoughts of Maggie, Tom, and Gerard, you are aware that each one attributes the failure of their magazine to the same root cause: a declining reader base. The audience for such a publication has not defected to the web. It is simply going extinct. Why then are they all leaping to the support of a project that is not going to solve the real problem?

In business literature, this phenomenon has come to be known as "groupthink." It's something of a misnomer. Something is going on here, but it can't properly be called *thinking*. Instead, what we are witnessing is a collective anxiety reaction. The survival of the organization is threatened. Like a herd of wildebeests, the members of

Team *Team Player* have all started to stampede in the same direction. Never mind whether it's the *right* direction. Where they are going is a lot less important at this point than the fact that they are all going there *together*.

It is almost a given that the solution adopted by an acutely anxious group will be the wrong one. To those faced with an immediate threat, the quick fix has overwhelming appeal, not because it's really a fix, but simply because it's quick. Acute anxiety produces a surge of physical energy that wants to DO SOMETHING. That Gwen's proposal is about to increase everyone's workload is actually part of its appeal. To act diminishes anxiety while to reflect may at least temporarily increase it. In reflecting, the group would have to face the fact that their magazine is becoming obsolete. This is the root problem, and it cannot be addressed without radical rethinking of their whole enterprise. If the root problem was not discussed under less-threatening circumstances, then it is even less likely to be discussed now that the group has become acutely anxious.

But why *wasn't* it discussed before it evolved into a crisis? The clues to this riddle have already been offered in the story you have read thus far.

First there is the parent company's sentimental attachment to the magazine as its founding publication. (If you were an employee of Heinz, would you want to be the one to suggest that the company should stop making ketchup?) A bright solution would be to revamp the magazine to target a different audience. But anyone who raised that solution would, in the very act of doing so, be openly admitting what no one wants to be the first to say aloud: that the current magazine is failing. That is the proverbial elephant on the conference table—something everyone can see but nobody refers to.

Secondly, and perhaps less obviously, the team has become crippled by all of Gwen's well-meaning team-building efforts. These rituals have repeatedly instilled her expectation and desire that they all feel and act as one. The task they are supposed to accomplish as a team has become secondary to team-ness, in and of itself. The initiative of each member is constrained by the need to coordinate what he or she is doing with what every other member is doing, and to bring his or her thinking in line with what the others are thinking.

Consider the results of the circus teambuilding retreat. The leader was good at facilitating communication about emotions and personality differences. The ability to handle personality conflicts with grace and humor persisted after the retreat and became a source of group self-esteem. They really do handle personality conflicts well. The trouble is that the problems facing them have nothing to do with personalities. Maggie, for instance, observes accurately that advertising clutter has compromised the quality of the magazine. This would be true no matter who was in charge of advertising sales, for it is a natural outcome of trying to keep revenues up as subscriptions dwindle. But no sooner does Maggie articulate this clear thought than she feels guilty. She attributes it to her own personality, her tendency to be a hypercritical "knife thrower." Maggie may indeed be hypercritical, but in this instance, she is also *right*.

Similarly, Tom sees that the sales department's problems are linked to the poor performance of the circulation department. This is important factual information. But he believes that in pointing it out, he is putting down a teammate toward whom he feels sympathetic. He knows that in Gerard's place, he probably couldn't do much better. Because he doesn't want to criticize Gerard personally, he avoids discussing a problem that is objectively occurring in Gerard's department.

The way I am describing this may give the impression that Maggie and Tom have made a conscious choice to sacrifice their objective assessment of the problem to group solidarity. In reality, that's not how the phenomenon is usually experienced. Emotionally, the individual fuses with the group so that a threat to the group is felt as if it were a threat to the self. If that threat arises from the self's own thinking, then thinking itself becomes, in a sense, the outsider, the threat. The thinker is a traitor not only to the group but also to the self who is identified with the group. To the extent that individuals fuse with the group, they will tend to reject any of their own thoughts that might unsettle the group. Thus, the group tends to congeal around the least provocative and original ideas of its members. This is how an organization composed of highly intelligent individuals can be, collectively, kind of dumb.

Still, the team functioned very effectively at the paintball retreat. Why? Because the objective of winning a paintball game had nothing to do with their everyday job objectives. The group was able to discuss their paintball strategy with each other quite openly, even heatedly at times, because the outcome was unimportant and raised no anxiety. The leader had chosen to build the retreat around paintball precisely *because* it was non-threatening. It did indeed heighten their pleasurable sense of togetherness but left unexplored the much more pertinent question of how, as individuals, they deal with anxiety. When an actual threat appeared, they instinctively sought comfort in that former sensation of togetherness. As they prepare to rush like lemmings off the fatal cliff of *Team Player Today: the e-zine*, at least they have each other for company.

Doodling, Daydreaming, and the Blahs

In stressful situations, it is commonplace for a group to congratulate itself on its sense of togetherness. You will hear people say, "This crisis has made us stronger." During the turbulent 1960s, many looked back with nostalgia to World War II when patriotism was fervent and uncomplicated, and Americans, united against a common threat, were not at odds with one another. The bond that a group experiences when it is under external attack feels cozy. The ease with which agreement is reached in a state of emergency makes everyone wonder why they can't always come together so harmoniously. It is objectively true that when faced with a serious external threat, groups tend to be at their most cooperative. What may be less obvious is that the later breakdown in cohesiveness that makes everyone a little nostalgic for the crisis is a natural consequence of the original fusion.

As far as we know, individual wildebeests don't feel weird about being just part of the herd. But you are not a wildebeest. As an intelligent individual human, when you glom together with a group, you start to feel a little weird. At first it seems wonderful. You feel like you finally belong. There is something almost romantic about it, something akin to falling in love. But then, little by little, you start to become irritated. You have more and more of those little thoughts that make you feel like a traitor, only you don't fully think them. You immediately suppress them. All these unacknowledged thoughts simmering under the surface make you feel a bit indisposed. You become restless and long to get away. If it is not practical to distance yourself physically, then you do so psychologically. In a meeting, you may find yourself doodling or daydreaming. You respond to another's animated communications with a bland "uh-huh." You're there yet not there.

Strange as it may seem, this blah quality that creeps into close relationships is another expression of anxiety. If to express your differences with another person or with a group threatens your—or their—need for togetherness, then you may suppress your genuine responses or simply be unable to get in touch with them. You may call the feeling you have on these occasions "boredom." It is a symptom that you are distancing from a togetherness that has started to feel claustrophobic.

If two people in a relationship or all members of a group felt the need for closeness or the need for separateness at the exact same time, then it wouldn't be a problem. They would fall into a natural rhythm of coming together and moving apart. But individuals vary in the amount of togetherness and separateness they need, or can tolerate. When anxious, some of us are inclined to seek more closeness while others of us are inclined to want more distance. This difference in inclination becomes, in itself, a source of further anxiety.

Where the difference is marked, and falls into a consistent pattern, the person who seeks closeness is called the "pursuer" and his or her partner, the "distancer." The pursuer will say of the distancer that he or she (usually he) "has a problem with intimacy." Curiously enough, the problem of the distancer is not inability to get close. It is most often a tendency to fuse, to feel so identified with the other person that the only way to recover the sense of self is to withdraw. When he does, the pursuer becomes anxious and seeks to relieve this anxiety by getting closer. Being pursued makes the distancer more anxious, and he responds by withdrawing further.

In the workplace, different job functions require different levels of interaction or separateness for purely practical reasons. Maggie is an editor, a job requiring long periods of solitary concentration. She is not distancing when she closes her office door and lets all her calls bounce to voicemail. She is doing her job. Tom, as a salesman, is supposed to seek a lot of interaction. He's not being a pursuer when he spends the whole day talking to advertisers on the phone. Neither Tom's constant social initiatives nor Maggie's social withdrawal is anxiety driven. They are task-appropriate behaviors.

When anxiety enters the picture, you begin to see pursuit and distancing activities that exceed or contradict job requirements. A person seeks more or less interaction than the task at hand requires. Camille, a junior editor in Maggie's department, spends a large portion of her day making the rounds of other employees' offices, where she regales them with the latest episodes in her convoluted romantic life. This may signal no more than a mismatch between her naturally gregarious temperament and the solitary nature of her job. But Maggie reacts with irritation to a level of closeness that is uncomfortable for her. When she brusquely cuts off these social visits in an effort to concentrate on her own work, Camille becomes anxious and reacts by pursuing. She interrupts Maggie frequently with requests for feedback or clarification or permission or answers that could easily be found in reference books. The more brusquely Maggie responds, the more Camille seems to strain for further pretexts to interrupt. If Maggie, in her discomfort at being pursued, continues to distance more and more, then she may eventually fail to offer even the level of interaction that Camille should legitimately expect of her as supervisor. The degree of contact starts to be driven by their anxiety dance rather than by the objective requirements of their professional relationship.

Gerard manages a small group of subscription telemarketers, a job requiring a lot of social interaction. Being naturally outgoing, he is well suited to it. But he is anxious because his telemarketers are not doing well. The subscriber base is vanishing, and now his salespeople are supposed to offer these non-existent people the dubious benefit of an electronic version of a magazine they don't want in the first place. He can feel their frustration. Three out of four of them are recovering from alcoholism, as he is himself. He wants to offer them an experience of success, yet he is uneasily aware that he has recruited them into a job where success is unlikely. More and more, he finds himself shutting the door to his cubicle and drawing the blinds. Despite—or perhaps even because of—his concern for his workers, he distances himself. When he interacts with his staff, he begins to over-identify with them, to feel their emotions as if they were his own. He can't be effective in the role of boss if he over-identifies. Not knowing how to separate himself from the emotions of his staff, he simply avoids contact with them.

In the Friday meeting, Gerard had been quick to join the headlong rush to support Gwen's proposal. By the end of the day, he had managed to get himself quite fired up about it. This is another indication of how readily he fuses with others. But over the succeeding weeks, he comes down with a case of the blahs. Offering a companion website is not, as hoped, inducing more readers to subscribe. Sales are as sluggish as ever. That he could have predicted this, if he'd thought about it, is not something he wants to think about now. The gap between what he knows and what he and his teammates want to believe drains him of energy and commitment.

Tom is having a similar experience. He finds that while advertisers are cautiously enthusiastic about the website, the total amount they are willing to spend on reaching readers of *Team Player Today* has not increased. They are simply dividing their advertising dollars between the magazine and the web. He sees that the venture is headed toward the catastrophe of having to support two different products out of a revenue base that was not even adequate to support one. He, too, keeps plugging along, but with a growing sense of futility. As for Maggie, she's simply buried. Straining under the effort of producing additional editorial content without an increase in staff, she doesn't have time to think about the big picture.

Unable to tolerate the gap between what they privately know and the collective delusion they have agreed to embrace, all three team members are instinctively distancing themselves from each other. In their various ways, each is no longer "all there." This gives rise to a lot of snafus—crossed signals, missed deadlines, and so forth. (It is this internal chaos that is producing such uproar over at the Pronto Agency, which keeps having to adjust to changing directives and timeframes.) Gwen, sensing the emotional distance, goes into pursuit mode. She calls team meetings almost daily, at which she tries to rally the troops with patriotic speeches about the dire threat they face and how they will triumph over it if they just all "pull together as a team." The intensity of her longing for group cohesion only makes it more difficult for any of them to voice their growing reservations. Their faces get a little blanker with each speech. In response, the speeches get longer and more fervent. As a group, they have begun to greatly exceed the national per capita consumption of pizza.

The Case Against Consensus

It's easy to analyze human folly from the sidelines. So let's go ahead and do it. That is, after all, what this book is for—to give you the luxury of observing anxious systems that are not directly affecting you. What would Gwen do if she could see what you see about her situation?

If her staff is bright and resourceful enough to have come this far in executing a really bad plan, just imagine what they could do with a good one. They also have, among them, enough insight into the real problem to come up with a good plan. Gwen sabotaged this possibility at the first meeting by offering an immediate solution instead of encouraging a more open-ended discussion of the problem. She goes on sabotaging it by insisting that they continue to display enthusiasm for the ill-considered quick fix.

I'm sure it's by now completely obvious to you what Gwen might be doing instead. Those blank faces, that general sense of the blahs she perceives in team meetings, are a clue that her staff is distancing. This is one of the things people do when they have private reservations that they are afraid to voice in a group setting. To a skillful leader, this is the signal that individuals in the group need clear permission to articulate conflicting thoughts.

"But I *gave* them permission," Gwen interrupts me to protest. "I said, 'Tell me frankly what obstacles you see. It's important that we all communicate honestly about this.' Those were my exact words!"

That's true. Why didn't it work? If you'll turn back a few pages, you will find that almost in the same breath, she said, "We're a really tight team." Since, in their anxiety, the group was already longing to pull together, and since, in her own anxiety, Gwen very much wanted them to do so, those were the words they heard and believed. The invitation to dissent meant nothing to them. They didn't believe it for a minute. It is not that they believed dissent would be actively punished. Gwen may be seen in the Pronto Agency as "the client from hell," but her employees do not see her as "the boss from hell." What they see in that meeting is how vulnerable she feels, how much she wants to offer the solution that will save the magazine, how badly she wants them to affirm her solution. The herd has closed ranks to protect its most vulnerable member. They would call it "wanting to be supportive."

There are no motions Gwen could go through that would solve this dilemma. To offer a *convincing* invitation to dissent, a leader must first manage her own anxiety. As we discussed in the previous chapter, this means first of all admitting to oneself that one is anxious. If Gwen were to say to herself, in so many words, "I am afraid they won't like my plan," she could then go on to think clearly about this fear. She and I never discussed this, but let's imagine for a moment that we did.

I begin, "Why is it scary to think they won't like your plan?"

Gwen looks at me like I'm retarded. "It's my job to save their jobs. I'm the group leader. If I don't come up with a plan, who will?"

"So you believe that it is your responsibility as leader to have all the answers."

"Well, no. Not *all* of them. I'm not a micromanager. It's up to Maggie to work out the editorial details, and up to Tom to work out the sales angle, and...."

"And up to you to lead the charge, so to speak."

"Well, yeah. Of course."

"Even if you're all charging off the edge of cliff?"

"Well, I told you, that's what I'm afraid of!" Gwen says plaintively.

"What if we were to define your job a little differently? What if we said your job was to draw out the best thinking of your staff?"

"That's what I was trying to do."

"Did you succeed?"

Gwen mulls this over. "I don't honestly know. I get the feeling they're thinking something they're not saying. But I don't know how to make them say it."

"You can't. There is no way you can control what they choose to say. All you can do is get out of their way. In other words, stop what you are doing to inhibit them."

"I don't get it. How am I inhibiting them?"

"By telegraphing your anxiety. They can feel that you are afraid to hear what they might have to say."

"I can't help that. I *am* afraid. That's how I really feel."

"Sure. But let's focus on how you are transmitting that fear to your staff. What are you doing that shows them you're afraid?"

"I don't think I was letting on at all. I mean, my tone was very positive."

"But still, they knew, right?"

"Right."

"So how?"

"Maybe because I sounded *too* positive? I kept saying 'I'm sure we can pull this off' when, really, I'm not so sure at all."

"Right. You also presented them with your solution immediately after stating the problem. What do you think would have happened if you'd approached the meeting in a more exploratory vein?"

She ponders this for a moment. "I think we'd have talked and talked for hours and never really gotten anywhere. They probably do have lots of ideas, maybe even some good ones I haven't thought of. But I don't believe we'd come to a consensus anytime soon. And time is of the essence here."

Gwen has a good point. Achieving true consensus, even on the rare occasions when it is possible, is extremely time consuming. For that reason alone, it is seldom appropriate when a group is faced with an immediate and serious threat. What's more, we've seen that when a group is acutely anxious, their togetherness drive increases sharply. This does not, paradoxically, lead to genuine consensus. Instead it leads to a suppression of differences in quest of the *appearance* of consensus. If everyone officially agrees that a consensus has been reached, then it becomes extremely difficult to reopen the question later when group members start to have second thoughts.

A better strategy for a leader in Gwen's position is to state at the outset that she is going to make the final decision, present her own ideas and invite the group to offer—and debate—various options for her to consider. In the course of that discussion, she will have heard whatever reservations team members have expressed about the plan she finally advocates. She can even restate these reservations at the time she announces her decision. This communicates powerfully to the team that she knows her plan is not ideal and that it's okay to continue to talk about obstacles as they emerge. One surprising advantage of this approach is that dissenters are actually more likely to devote energy to the plan. Because they have not been pressured to go along with the group, they have less need to distance themselves. They are also in the enviable position of being able to say, "I told you so," if the plan doesn't work.

Reversing the Stampede

Gwen and I didn't have that conversation. Amazingly enough, Team *Team Player* managed to resolve their crisis without my intervention.

The surprising turn of events began during Gerard's weekly lunch date with Ben, his AA sponsor. He confided the stress he was feeling over current events at work, particularly his growing estrangement from his own staff.

"Well, there's that grandiosity thing again," Ben remarked, after letting him vent for a while.

"Yeah, I know. Thinking it's up to me to single-handedly save the planet. I just hate getting up every day to go through these exercises in futility. It's like we all know deep down that it isn't going to work, but no one has the nerve to say so. We just keep going through the motions."

"Well, as we say, 'God give me to serenity to accept what I can't change, the strength to change what I can—'"

"'—and the wisdom to know the difference.' Hey, wait a minute, Ben. I think I *do* know the difference. It just hit me. I can't control what subscribers do or what the team does or what becomes of the magazine or our jobs. But I can control whether I go on sitting there like a zombie in meetings. Here I am complaining that no one else speaks up. Well, why don't I?"

With that insight, Gerard differentiated himself from the emotional system with which he had become fused. He acknowledged his own anxiety and discovered, just beneath it, an I-position waiting to be born.

At the next team meeting, he waits till Gwen has finished her customary speech and everyone is on their second slice of pizza. Clearing his throat nervously, he begins, "Look, guys, I have a confession. I was the one who came up with the idea that a password-protected section of the website would be a great incentive to subscribers. I must have forgotten to pick up my brain from the cleaners the day I said that. It ain't happening. My guys have been pushing the thing like crazy, and we're still not getting anywhere near the numbers we need."

Gerard doesn't know what reaction he was expecting, but it wasn't the complete silence with which his teammates meet this admission. They're all staring at him dumbly, like they're expecting him to say more. He hasn't worked out what he will say next.

Finally Maggie comes to what she hopes will be the rescue. "Is there something we could be doing, content-wise, that will make your job easier, Gerard?"

He's about to say No when he gets a sudden inspiration. "You know that article you did last month on virtual assistants? I was kind of intrigued by that. Just when we're about to conclude that secretaries are a vanishing breed, then they start popping up again in a new form. That might be a new potential subscriber pool, but I'm not sure how to find them. Any ideas? Is there a virtual-assistant association or something like that?"

"Sorry," Tom breaks in. "I missed the article. What's a virtual assistant?"

"They're freelance personal secretaries who work out of their own homes," Maggie explains. "Their clients may be located anywhere in the world, and sometimes they've never even met them in the flesh. Most of them—the clients—are also home-based entrepreneurs. But it's a very new phenomenon. I don't think there are enough of them to make a dent in our circulation figures."

"That's what appeals to me about it, though," Gerard says. "It's *new*. It would be cool to get out in front of a growing trend for a change—"

"—instead of trying to squeeze the last bit of life out of a dying one," Maggie finishes. "Yeah. Tell me about it."

"Well, it's funny you should bring this up because I've been thinking something along the same lines," says Tom. "Our computer advertisers keep telling me home-office workers are their fastest growing source of sales. Self-employed people tend to buy themselves better systems than their former employers were willing to buy for them. They're also quicker to purchase upgrades. Anyway, the first thing these advertisers always ask is whether we reach any of this market, and I have to tell them No. It would be great to be able to tell them Yes."

"Well, like I say, there are only a handful of virtual assistants so far," says Maggie.

"I hear you. But what do all those other home-based workers do for clerical support?"

"Same thing most of us do. Muddle through some-how."

"Yeah, but if our computer breaks down, then the IT guy comes to fix it. There's somebody at the front desk to accept deliveries and someone else who comes to vacuum and empty the wastebaskets. There's a copy machine just down the hall, maintenance people to keep the air conditioning working, and so forth. When you think of it, even without secretaries, we still have a lot of support services that home workers don't have. They have to find people to provide at least some of those services. Do you see where I'm going with this? There's a whole new world of sponsors we could get if we were reaching that market. Can you see any way of doing that, editorially?"

"Not if we're calling it *Team Player Today*. I mean, obviously."

"What's the opposite of team player?" Gerard wonders aloud. "Lone wolf?"

"Lone Ranger?"

"Rugged Individualist?"

"Narcissist?"

"Selfish pig?"

"Wanker?"

Everyone laughs. Relief at opening up the forbidden topic has made them all a little punchy. (Humor, by the way, is a terrific strategy for defusing group anxiety.)

"How about 'My Way,'" Tom suggests. "I read somewhere that was voted the #1 song of the millennium."

"I love it!" Maggie exults. "You know the trouble with *Team Player Today* as a title is that, while no one wants to hear that they're *not* a team player, no one can get all that excited about thinking they *are* one, either. It's not something you can imagine Sinatra singing about." She avoids Gwen's eyes as she says this, hardly believing her own nerve.

"Kind of goody-goody," Gerard agrees. "With 'My Way' you're talking the hopes and dreams of the self-employed. As soon as you say the name, you've got 'em hooked. Now *that's* something that would make my job a whole lot easier." He pauses to muster his courage before pushing on. "So where are we going with this? Are we just shooting the breeze here, or are we talking about launching a new product?"

"Since we're basically starting from scratch with the website anyhow, why not launch something *really* new?" suggests Tom.

"You mean keep the magazine the same but target the website to home workers?" Maggie asks.

"Yeah. Something like that."

"Editorially, there wouldn't be that much overlap. It's like asking me to produce two entirely different publications with no additional staff. Puh-leeze."

"You're right. I guess it was a crazy idea."

"No, I'm not saying that. I like it, actually. I mean, the My Way idea. It opens up whole new areas of content. It'd be a blast. I just can't see doing it at the same time we're trying to keep *Team Player* afloat."

"What if we don't bother?" Gerard suggests. "What if we just let the old gal die a dignified death?"

Everyone glances nervously at Gwen, waiting for her to say, "A quitter never wins," or "I expect you all to step up to the puck and hit it all the way to the eighteenth hole." But Gwen is just chewing thoughtfully on the end of her Cola straw, waiting for them to continue.

"I'm for it," Maggie says. "Gerard, I'd like to hear your impressions of this, but it seems to me our problem is not just that there are fewer clericals than in the past. It's that people who take these jobs no longer look at being a secretary as a long-term career choice. It's a steppingstone to something else. In other words, they don't want to identify too strongly with the job, and that's why they don't care to read a magazine about it."

"That's hitting it on the head, Maggie. I would have said it earlier, but I didn't want to mess with your morale."

The meeting went on for the rest of the afternoon. By the time it was finished, the team had agreed to stop producing *Team Player Today* and were well into the planning of the *My Way* launch. Tom had a long list of new advertisers to pursue; Maggie, a long list of feature ideas; and Gwen was busy planning her pitch to the parent company. Gerard was still reeling in amazement at how easy it had been.

Are you surprised too? If fear is contagious, then so is courage. In an anxious organization, a single individual can have a powerful and wide-ranging effect just by mastering his or her own anxiety. When Gerard had the nerve to name "the elephant on the conference table," everyone was vastly relieved, for it had been making everyone chronically anxious for years. Finally naming it liberated all the energy that had been tied up in the effort of ignoring it. As their anxiety dissipated somewhat, they were all able to think more clearly. As a promising solution emerged from that thinking, their anxiety dissipated even further. Gwen was able to drop her pursuer role because her staff was fully present for a change. They in turn felt freer to express themselves as individuals when she stopped exhorting them to feel like a team. Oddly enough, what this particular group had been suppressing was not conflict but agreement. Each person's private "traitor thought" turned out to be the same as those of their teammates. The effort of pretending to agree with a fiction had kept them from discovering their genuine point of agreement.

It's not always this easy, as you will discover when we return to the Pronto Agency. But sometimes it is.

One more thing before the newly inaugurated Team *My Way* departs for happy hour....Maybe you've been wondering what the deal is with Gwen. When she appeared in earlier chapters as a Pronto client, she was the dragon lady. Here, on her own turf, she's more like a cross between Yogi Berra and Mama Bear. What gives? The point this illustrates is that behavior is contextual. How a person acts is, to a great extent, shaped by the social system he or she is in. There is, however a common thread to Gwen's anxiety reactions with her own team and the Pronto staff. We will be exploring that in a later chapter.

In Summary...

 When faced with an immediate threat, a group will tend to gravitate toward the quick fix. It is seldom truly a fix but has overwhelming appeal because it is quick.

 When anxiety runs high, togetherness pressures within a group may increase. Emotionally, the individual fuses with the group so that a threat to the group is felt as if it were a threat to the self. To the extent that individuals fuse with the group, they will tend to reject any of their own thoughts that might unsettle the group. Without even articulating it, the group will collectively agree to avoid discussing facts and issues that raise anxiety.

 The suppression of individual differences and reluctance to discuss unsettling subjects leads to an overall loss of energy in a group. Rather than risk self-expression, members begin to subtly distance themselves. Boredom and irritability are symptoms of this phenomenon.

 People vary in the amount of closeness and distance they prefer. When anxious, "pursuers" crave and actively seek greater closeness while "distancers" feel the need to withdraw. This difference in inclination can become a source of anxiety in relationships.

 Achieving consensus requires both time and candid discussion. It is rarely possible or desirable when a group is faced with an acute threat. In such circumstances the tendency to go along with the group increases, resulting in a suppression of differences and a false appearance of consensus.

Chapter 4

Three's Company

The triangle as the basic unit
of organizational politics

N ow let's see how it's going with Steve, the graphic design manager at Pronto. When we last saw him, he was getting ready to take an I-position. He had decided that he would no longer accept last-minute work assignments from account executives if it meant having to ask employees to work over-time without advance notice.

Realizing that his position was likely to displease the account executives, Steve thought carefully about how to present it to them. At the next meeting of the management staff, he began by pointing out that unpredictable overtime demands are putting stress on the designers and contributing to high staff turnover. He explained that he could reduce stress without cutting workload by enabling the designers to better predict and control their schedules. To that end, he had studied the current workflow and determined realistic lead times for each of the services his department provides. He passed out a list of these lead times and asked the account executives to consult it when planning client campaigns. He added that while it may on occasion be possible to provide speedier service, they should check with him before promising this to clients.

To his relief and amazement, the meeting went well. No one complained. The CEO nodded with seeming approval, and Jennifer, one of the account execs, even went so far as to say, "Thanks, Steve. I've never been sure what to tell clients about timeframes before. This will be a help." Encouraged by this apparent success, he went on to announce the change to his staff, who were naturally quite pleased. At the end of the day, he called me in a state of jubilation. "This was so much easier than I thought it would be. I don't know why I didn't think of doing it earlier." I refrained from telling him that he was about to find out.

A week later, while packing up to leave for the day, Steve notices that Cheri is still at her workstation, making a frantic call to her babysitter. When he asks what's up, she explains that Susan called around 4 p.m., imploring her to revise a magazine ad by 9 a.m. the following morning.

"This is news to me," Steve says.

"Yeah, I know. Susan called me directly. Said if she asked you, you'd probably say No. She sounded really desperate. You know how she is."

Steve takes a six-second vacation, trying to control his fury. With all the calmness he can muster, he says, "In the future, please tell Susan that all work assignments come through me."

Cheri shrugs. "Well, while you two slug it out, I'm just going to take the path of least resistance, okay?"

The following morning, he tells Susan the same thing. He is pleasant but firm. She replies, "I know, I know...." and then launches into a melodramatic tale of the desperate and beyond-her-control circumstances that had motivated her. She promises not to let it happen again.

Two days later Susan bursts into Steve's office, looking even more wired than usual. "You're not going to believe this! I thought I'd heard everything, but this takes the cake. Guess what our favorite client has done now."

"I'll bite."

"Changed the name of *Team Player Today*. Now they're calling it *My Way*."

"As in 'or the highway'?"

Susan laughs shrilly. "You think I'm kidding, but I'm not. They've changed title, market, content—basically everything but the deadline. All the design templates will have to be redone, and they want to see it by Monday."

"That isn't possible," Steve says calmly. "Even under the best of circumstances, a new graphic identity takes a couple of weeks. And we're swamped right now."

"Yes, I appreciate that it's tight, but we've gotta do it," Susan insists. "Gwen's on the war path again. You know how she is—type A all the way. There's just no reasoning with her. Please, I need you to work with me on this one, Steve."

Steve mentally reviews the current workload and concludes that he can't accommodate her without inflicting heavy overtime demands on his staff. He is so reluctant to refuse that he considers doing the job himself, but a major project for Jennifer, due Friday, is already going to have him burning the midnight oil. Finally he attempts to compromise, offering a timeframe that's too short for his comfort and too long for Susan's. "A week from Friday. It's honestly the best I can do, and even that is going to be a squeeze."

"I can't live with that."

"I'm afraid you're going to have to."

Though Susan is pouting as she leaves his office, Steve is rather pleased with himself for holding firm.

Later that evening, as he is racing to get ahead on Jennifer's job, Irv, the CEO drops by his office, bearing a large café latte. "Thought you could use refueling," he says pleasantly. They chitchat for a few minutes before Irv comes round to his real business. "Susan has told me you're pretty jammed up this week, but if you could see your way clear to finishing the My Way job by Monday...well, I would consider it a personal favor. Gwen is really breathing down my neck on this one. Causes me more stress than all our other clients combined."

Steve reaches hastily for a pile of napkins to mop up the café latte he's just spilled all over his desk. His thoughts about Susan at this moment are unprintable. Not knowing what else to do, he assents. He has to pull two staff members off other projects, ask them to stay late every night, *and* pitch in himself besides. As a result, they make Susan's deadline but miss Jennifer's.

"I hate doing this to you, Jen," he apologizes. "Especially since you've been so great about working with our lead times. It's just that Susan went crying to Irv, and he moved her job to the head of the queue. My hands were tied."

Jennifer accepts his apology with pretty good grace but adds, "I guess it pays to be the squeaky wheel around here."

Anxiety Breeds Triangles

The technical term for what Steve is experiencing is "pushback." When one member of a system takes a position that disrupts the anxiety ecology, the system pushes back. Ideally, Steve's position would prompt the account executives to assert realistic time-frames when negotiating with clients, and this was indeed Jennifer's response. The clarity of Steve's position actually reduced her anxiety because she knew what to expect from him and had no great difficulty adjusting to that expectation. But for Susan, taking a firm position with clients raises too much anxiety. Instead, she pushes back.

Let's take a closer look at the form this pushback is taking. Steve's I-position has presented Susan with a problem that she feels unable to resolve by confronting him directly. Instead, she draws in third parties. First she goes behind his back to make a request of Cheri. She tries to enlist Cheri's sympathy by admitting she's afraid to ask Steve directly. She creates a triangle: Susan and Cheri versus Steve. When Steve nips this in the bud, she draws in Gwen, trying to persuade him that the two of them must team up to cope with the difficult client: Steve and Susan versus Gwen. When the results of that are not fully satisfactory, she creates another triangle with Irv: Susan and Irv versus Steve.

What Susan is doing is called "triangling." (Yes, we're using "triangle" as a verb.) She is drawing in one person to relieve the anxiety in a relationship with another person. As you are about to discover, everybody does this.

Like a two-legged stool, a one-on-one relationship is inherently unstable. This instability is relieved by drawing in another party, a third leg. Sometimes the third party is triangled in when one or both people in a relationship are feeling too close for comfort. The excess of intimacy is, in effect, spread out. Conversely, triangling can be used to create a sense of closeness that is lacking. It is also used to manage conflict.

Steve was triangling when he complained to Rocky about Susan in the employee lounge. He and Susan had a conflict and, as neither will confirm that the other's position is valid, Steve seeks confirmation from a third party. Some of the tension in Steve's relationship with Susan is dispelled for him by triangling Rocky into it. But here's an interesting twist: at the same time, Susan is being triangled in to dispel the anxiety in the relationship between Steve and Rocky. Though they are professional peers, they have little in common on a personal level. If they met outside of work, they would not likely become friends, and when they run into each other at the office, making small talk is an effort for them both. Being fed up with Susan is one of the few things they can heartily agree on. Griping about her brings them closer. It gives them something to talk about besides the weather.

There are additional triangles in the anecdote with which I began this chapter. Before reading further, see if you can spot them for yourself.

When Irv, having been triangled into Susan's conflict with Steve, attempts to intercede for Susan, he triangles Gwen into his relationship with Steve. He tries to win Steve over to his side by reminding him what a demanding client Gwen is.

When Steve faces a potential conflict with Jennifer over missing her deadline, he triangles in Susan. He seeks Jennifer's commiseration with the difficult position Susan has placed him in. Meanwhile Jennifer, learning that Irv has bumped her job in favor of Susan's, is now in an Irv-Susan-Jennifer triangle.

As you can see, the anxiety with which the system has responded to Steve's I-position has so far resulted in at least six different triangles. As it continues to spread, even more triangles will be created. For instance, now that Jennifer is in conflict with Susan, she is likely to seek an ally. Cheri, in her discomfort at being drawn into a triangle with Susan and Steve, has probably triangled with a co-worker, family member, or friend. As these triangles proliferate, the anxiety travels to more and more people who were not a part of the original conflict. This also serves to spread the anxiety thinner. Instead of two acutely anxious people, you have an indeterminate number of mildly anxious people.

The Relationship Tripod

Triangles are the basic unit of any relationship system. Analyze how people relate in any organization and you will find a pattern of interlocking triangles.

Why is the basic unit a triangle and not a twosome? Consider what happens when you fall in love. In the beginning, all you and your partner want to think about is each other. You start to complete each other's sentences. But as time wears on, each of you starts to feel a little bit uncomfortable. In the fusion that occurs between you, you begin to lose your sense of self. You start to wish you could complete your own sentences. As you attempt to distance, irritability and/or boredom may set in. Then you start to feel anxious because "the romance is wearing off." This tension between closeness and distance makes the twosome inherently unstable. It is resolved by introducing a third element. An example of this is a couple who believes that having a child will save their marriage. Ordinarily, though, the solution is far less drastic. The pair seeks a third element by drawing in another person—a friend, family member, or a shared adversary.

As any three people can form a triangle, the number of potential triangles in an organization can be astronomical. In a group of four people, there are four potential triangles. Add a fifth person and ten triangles are possible. If we confine the cast of characters at Pronto to the seven already named—Irv, Susan, Steve, Rocky, Jennifer, Cheri, and Gwen—there are thirty-five potential triangles. A company of fifty people yields 19,600 while a company of 500 people yields over twenty million!

All of these triangles are *theoretically* possible in that all of these people come into contact with each other. Yet not all of them may be activated, leading to the phenomenon we are calling "triangling." Suppose that Rocky is writing the copy for one of Jennifer's projects and Cheri is designing the layout. Meeting as a threesome to discuss the job is not necessarily triangling. A triangle is not activated unless anxiety comes into the situation. Say, for example, that Rocky and Cheri cannot agree on the creative approach to take. As they argue their positions, they keep glancing over at Jennifer to see if she agrees. That's a triangle. Or suppose Cheri is having trouble making the copy fit and complains to Jennifer that Rocky has written too much. That, too, is a triangle.

You are probably getting the impression from what has been said so far that triangling is bad. Certainly it *felt* bad to Steve when Susan triangled with Cheri and Irv. At its worst, the triangle is the basic shape of every betrayal—from gossip to marital infidelity to criminal conspiracy. To counteract the impression that it is therefore the root of all evil, let's look at triangles in some of their more benign forms:

▶ After a stressful interaction with a difficult customer, you rant about him to a co-worker. The co-worker sympathizes and maybe says something that makes you laugh. Triangling has dissipated the anger you felt toward the customer and perhaps also strengthened the bond you feel with your colleague.

▶ You and your spouse have been vacationing together for a week and are beginning to get on each other's nerves. You invite another couple you've just met to have dinner with you. Their presence dispels the tension of too much togetherness, and during dinner you and your spouse feel more relaxed with each other. After the other couple departs, you discuss them together, and this gives you an enjoyable sense of closeness.

▶ You are on the verge of closing a big sale when the customer confides that she is having trouble getting approval from her boss. Together you explore the possible reasons for his resistance and work out a strategy for overcoming it.

▶ You're in a sports bar and feel like socializing, but you don't know the guy sitting next to you and aren't sure how to start a conversation. On the TV overhead, your team is losing badly. You and your neighbor launch into a lively discussion of what the coach ought to be doing about it.

As these examples demonstrate, triangles are perfectly natural and often downright beneficial. Yet when I describe the triangles being activated in our latest visit to the Pronto Agency, your stress level probably rises just reading about them. As with other anxiety-containment mechanisms, triangling can end up making matters a whole lot worse. Instead of merely dissipating anxiety, triangling can create more of it. Let's look at some of the variables that lead to this unwanted result.

The first time Steve and Rocky griped together about Susan, their exchange was lively. They laughed a lot, and they both came out of it feeling a little better. But engaging in the same behavior again and again does not continue to have this stress-relieving effect. Instead it begins to make the problem seem more formidable. If we are talking about this every day, then it must be a really big deal. If we talk about it every day and never see a solution, then it must be unsolvable. A feeling of heaviness sets in. The thrill is gone. Talking about Susan begins to feel like a habit, and nothing really new is being said. The laughter starts to ring a little hollow, and when the topic of Susan is exhausted for the present, an uncomfortable lull arises in the conversation. Rocky and Steve are not sure what to talk about instead.

Suppose Rocky has an interaction with Susan that turns out to be rather delightful. Is he likely to tell Steve about it? Probably not. Their sense of togetherness is based on having a shared adversary. If one of them gets friendly with the adversary, then the other will become anxious. Triangling that was helpful the first time they did it gradually turns problematic because they *keep* doing it—and because they don't do much else in relationship to each other.

In organizations, some of the problems that seem really solid and intractable are little more, at root, than the constant conversational material of people who don't know what else to say to each other. Griping about a certain person, department, or policy has become like talking about the weather. It is a problem mainly because the speakers have tacitly agreed to keep referring to it as The Problem. To suggest that it isn't such a big problem after all is to set oneself apart and threaten the togetherness. In a sense, The Problem is holding relationships together, and that's why no one is particularly invested in solving it.

In the Steve-Rocky-Susan triangle, there is no movement. Steve and Rocky are the insiders and Susan, the outsider. It stays like that, week after week. In other triangles, the insider/outsider configuration may shift, and each shift raises the anxiety of at least one party. When Steve wanted to rescue Cheri from the unfair demands of Susan, he was feeling himself to be in a triangle in which he and Cheri were the insiders and Susan the outsider. But the evening he found Cheri staying late, it seemed the triangle had shifted. Susan had gotten Cheri to make a commitment that he didn't know about, and she had done this by confiding to Cheri that she was afraid to approach Steve. In that moment, Susan and Cheri were the insiders, and Steve was the outsider.

When that happened, Steve had a vague sense of having been betrayed. This is how we usually feel when we are pushed into the outside position of a triangle in which we previously enjoyed an inside position. If a spouse or lover is unfaithful, then this sense of betrayal may be huge, for we have been moved to an outside position in a relationship where we hoped we could always count on remaining on the inside. But almost every day we experience shifts far too subtle for a melodramatic word like "betrayal." Often the shift is so subtle that we don't even register that we are feeling rejected. We just have a vague feeling of discomfort or uneasiness that we can't quite put our fingers on. Steve would say that he was annoyed that Susan "did an end run" around his deadline policy. "Doing an end run," "going over my head," and "being left out of the loop" are phrases used in business settings to express discomfort with the outside position in a triangle.

Steve found himself in the outsider position again when Susan triangled with Irv. It was, as he experienced it, a little conspiracy between the two of them to override his deadline needs. But with his next words, Irv moves Steve to the insider position in an Irv-Steve-Gwen triangle. He and Irv are on the inside, ostensibly agreeing that Gwen is the problem. Steve doesn't actually have anything against Gwen, yet there is some comfort in being back on the inside with Irv—even if it's the inside of a different triangle. This rapid shift is part of what flustered Steve. It would not have been easy in any case to refuse the request of the CEO, but at that moment Steve couldn't even think straight about whether he *wanted* to refuse. The one-two punch of threat (being the outsider in an Irv triangle) and relief (being on the inside of another Irv triangle) disoriented him. If this were a conscious manipulation on Irv's part, it would be diabolically effective. But Irv, like most of us, is not conscious that he is triangling. From his point of view, he's coping as best he can with the anxiety of having been triangled by Susan into the conflict between her and Steve.

When conflict in a triangle is intense, the role of outsider becomes the more desirable position. This is the role Cheri was seeking when she said, "You two go ahead and slug it out." Being triangled into the conflict between Susan and Steve was causing her stress, and she wanted to distance herself from it.

Jennifer has a similar response to being triangled into the Susan-Steve conflict. At first, her reaction is to take an inside position with Steve by calling Susan "the squeaky wheel." This is especially tempting to her because she is annoyed with Susan. But on further reflection, she realizes that her problem cannot be resolved by siding with either one of them. Instead, she casually mentions to Irv that she wishes Susan and Steve could work things out because their "communication gap" has started to impact other account executives' projects. In doing so she takes the outside position in the Steve-Susan-Jennifer triangle.

The Perils of Peacekeeping

Irv has already observed that there is tension between Susan and Steve and decides he'd better do something about it. The next time he has a moment alone with Susan, he says, "You know, Steve is making a valiant effort to bring some order to the work flow in the graphics department. Try to work with him on that, will you?" In a private moment with Steve, he says, "You know, Susan is in the unenviable position of having to work with our most demanding client. Most of these emergencies that keep cropping up are beyond her control. Maybe you can cut her some slack now and then."

Irv has read somewhere that if you praise people for what they're not doing yet, then they'll start to do it. At the next meeting of the management team, he gives this strategy a try. He announces that the client is very pleased with the *My Way* website and congratulates Susan and Steve for having worked so effectively together to bring about this happy result. "This is the kind of teamwork that puts Pronto head and shoulders above the competition," he concludes. Inwardly, he congratulates himself for his tactful mediation. He feels like he has shown the wisdom of Solomon in dealing with them both so even handedly.

I'm afraid I'll have to burst his bubble. If Susan and Steve were six-year-olds, they'd have been punching each other in the arm at that meeting and hissing, "You started it!" "No, *you* started it!" Adults don't say this. They just think it. Irv's intervention has demonstrated that he is aware of the friction between them and that he wants it to stop. No matter how tactfully he conveys it, the emotional message they get is that they are "in trouble" for not getting along. This does not make them the least bit more motivated to get along in the future. The conflict only becomes more solid now that it has been tacitly acknowledged by Irv. It is an official Problem. This increases the anxiety between them. His private remarks give each of them the impression that Irv has taken the other's side. Both want to scream "Unfair!"

This is what happens when one person attempts to mediate a conflict between two others. It doesn't work. The mediator may bask in a self-bestowed "blessed are the peacemakers" halo, but the actual effect is typically to create a new triangle in which the mediator occupies an uncomfortable outside position. The only thing the combatants can agree on is that the mediator is their common adversary.

So what are you supposed to do if two members of your staff are at each other's throats? Continue to relate to each as an individual but do nothing about the conflict itself. It is not your job to make them like each other. It is not your job to make them happy. If you stop to think about it, this wish comes from the anxiety their conflict is causing *you*. Recall how Gwen's wish for a cohesive team could be felt by her entire staff. Recall how it affected them. Her anxious desire that everyone agree actually delayed their coming to genuine agreement.

When conflicts interfere with job performance, bosses are within their rights in stating performance expectations. If Irv says to Steve, "I expect you to accept Susan's last-minute assignments," that's a legitimate performance expectation. It's what Steve is being paid to do. But cutting someone slack or feeling sympathy for their predicament are not things that you can pay a person to do. How employees feel is their own business.

Ironically, Irv made an illegitimate demand ("Cut Susan some slack") instead of a legitimate one ("Accept her last-minute assignments") because he didn't want to take sides. He thought he was being respectful of them in leaving them to work it out rather than throwing the weight of his authority to one side or the other. But it is actually the ambiguity of Irv's position that is perpetuating the conflict. Susan believes her demands are reasonable. Steve believes they're not. There is, at present, no independent standard against which either of them can judge the matter, so they are trying to resolve it in a battle of wills.

Recall what we talked about in Chapter 2. If a situation is making you anxious, then there's a question in there somewhere that is yours alone to answer. The question is not about personalities but about principles. For Irv that question is, "Where do I stand on the issue of last minute-work assignments? Am I willing to take the consequences to the agency of supporting the policy Steve has proposed?" Whether Irv will ever get around to answering that question is a cliffhanger we'll leave for a later chapter.

Managing Yourself in Triangles

Are you finding all this a bit depressing? The impression given by this chapter is that workplace relationships are an endless series of interlocking triangles in which each person is jockeying for position. Each person is being subtly—or, in some cases, not so subtly—manipulated by triangles that are sometimes set up by a single careless sentence. Perhaps this is striking you as a rather cold and mechanistic view of human behavior.

What I hope to get across is that what you're finding repellant in this chapter is the very thing that's making you anxious at work. We are renaming the beast that you're probably used to calling "office politics." Coming to understand the instincts of the beast is your best hope of taming it. The process begins with what Harriet Lerner calls "thinking in threes." When the personal or political dynamics of a work situation become bewildering, you can get a conceptual handle on what's going on by looking for the triangles. Learning to manage your own behavior in triangles is probably the single most important thing you can learn about handling workplace politics.

The fundamentals of triangling should give you some pretty good insights into the structure of whatever mess you happen to be in. But how do you get out of it?

That's what Steve wanted to know the next time we met. We sketched out all of the significant triangles he was a part of and identified his current position in each. As a graphic artist, he related well to this exercise. "Cool," he said, admiring his neatly labeled diagram of interlocking triangles. "Looks a bit like a cyclone fence. That's what it feels like, too. A cyclone *and* a fence. I feel totally fenced in by the whole thing. Any way to get rid of some of these triangles?"

"Yes. What you can do is manage your own behavior in such a way that you diminish both your own anxiety and that of others. You've already shown that you know how to do this."

Steve looks at me blankly. "I do?"

"Sure. The first time we met, you were telling me about a triangle you were in with Cheri and Susan. Remember? You wanted to rescue Cheri from the cruel and unusual overtime demands of Susan."

"Which you convinced me was a lousy idea."

"Right. So what did you do instead?"

"Well, the next thing that happened was that I took my legendary I-Position," Steve says, rolling his eyes. "That was sure a whopping success."

"Yes, it was," I say seriously. "You got clear on where you stand, and so did everyone around you. You stopped seeing the thing in terms of personalities and viewed it instead in terms of issues. It was no longer a matter of punishing Susan or rescuing Cheri. On an emotional level, at least, you got yourself detriangled from that one."

"Yeah, and it felt great. For about a day. Then Susan triangled me right back in."

"Right. So let's look at what you did next. As I recall, you talked to Cheri first. What did you say?"

"I told her that all job assignments were supposed to come through me."

"Did that need saying?"

"What do you mean?"

"I mean, was that new information for Cheri?"

"It shouldn't have been. I've said it all along, and I reiterated it when I announced the new overtime policy."

"So Cheri knew—or at least had reason to know—that she could have gotten out of Susan's request by reminding her of the policy. Instead she chose to accept the job. She was staying late of her own free choice."

"I never thought of that, but you're right. Yeah. But I hate how Susan got her to do that. It was manipulative."

"Is that your problem?"

"I seem to be *making* it my problem."

"Exactly. And that's how you got triangled back in. You made yourself responsible for sorting out what was happening between two other people."

"Okay, yeah. But you're missing something. The real issue was that I don't want account executives making work assignments to my staff without consulting me first. Period."

"A position that you stated firmly to Susan; am I right?"

"Right."

"And that, if I'm not mistaken, she has honored ever since."

"You're right! I kind of overlooked that because of the hassle that came up afterwards. It all seemed like one big problem to me. Still does. The problem of Susan not respecting my needs."

"Sure. When you look at it in terms of personalities, it's always the same basic clash. But if you see it in terms of issues, you have actually managed to settle one of those issues. Whether or not she respects your needs, Susan has abided by one of your requests."

"So it's a matter of continuing to state I-positions? That's how you get detriangled?"

"In principle, yes. Absolutely. Take sides with issues, not personalities, and state your position clearly. That's necessary, but as you can see, it is not always sufficient. There are two other things you need to address. The first is looking at the objective situation that is giving rise to the triangle in the first place. What problem is Susan trying to solve with all this triangling she's been doing?"

"She can't live with my position on timeframes. Or at least she doesn't want to."

"So there's a conflict between what she wants and what you want, and no clear way to break the tie. In that situation, people almost inevitably go looking for a third party to take their side."

"I didn't," Steve said huffily.

"You didn't have to. At the point Susan triangled in Irv, you were getting your way."

"True. But now he's taken her side, and I'm screwed."

"Well that brings me to the other point that needs to be addressed. When you are in a triangle, it is important to maintain a one-on-one relationship with each of the other two parties, independently of the other."

"I did have a separate conversation with Irv. That's when he took her side."

"Or at least appeared to. Did Irv state to you his position on this issue?"

"He asked me to meet her deadline."

"Sure. But is that his considered position? It sounds to me more like a reaction. The immediate situation—not only with Susan but also with the client—was making him anxious, and he reached for a quick fix."

"The net effect was the same. How can I maintain my position if the CEO is going to undercut it like that?"

"You can't. Have you discussed this with Irv?"

"Not in so many words, no. I guess what you're saying is, I'd better. Yeah, I guess I'd better. Yikes. You didn't warn me how complicated this was going to get. It seems like when I took my I-position, everything got worse."

"What has happened is that you transformed chronic anxiety into acute anxiety. That might not sound like an improvement, but unless you turn up the heat on issues that are causing chronic anxiety, they tend never to be addressed. What you're seeing now is an attempt of your organization to return to its habitual state of chronic anxiety. Triangling is how it's done. If you triangle in enough people, the anxiety gets spread out to a level where everyone finds it tolerable and nothing changes"

Steve looks perplexed. "Maybe I don't get what you're saying. It seems to me that involving more people does turn up the heat. I mean, more people are affected by the problem so that there's greater pressure for a solution. Isn't there?"

"Unless all those people have a major stake in your issue, that's not going to work. Because what they really have a stake in is reducing the anxiety of the group. Involve the group as a whole, or many of its members, and what's likely to happen is that you'll be pressured into a compromise that won't satisfy you *or* Susan. The group will just want to get the conflict over with as soon as possible."

We'll leave Steve to ponder that last point for now. Meanwhile, let me quickly recapitulate what I told him about getting detriangled. Appropriately, there are three steps. They are as follow:

1. Look for the objective trigger of the anxiety that has led the triangle to arise.

2. Side with issues, not people. Take an I-position.

3. Maintain an independent relationship with each of the other members of the triangle.

In Summary...

 Any relationship between two people will seek to stabilize itself by triangling in a third person. If you want to better understand what's going on between you and someone else, then look for that third person.

 If the relationship between two people is harmonious (in other words, if the anxiety between them is low), then the third person will be the outsider. They are using that person either to create more closeness (by excluding the outsider) or to create more distance (by giving the relationship something outside of itself to focus on). Often they are doing both.

 The outsider will usually be trying to move to an inside position. This can only be done by displacing one of the inside members. The anxiety of the targeted inside member will increase.

 When there is conflict between two people, either or both of them may be seeking to win the third person over to his or her side. If this occurs, then that person becomes an insider and the "loser" in the conflict becomes the outsider.

When conflict and anxiety in a triangle are high, the outside position becomes more desirable.

 If your situation seems to include more than three players, then you are dealing with a system of interlocking triangles. These additional triangles are spawned when anxiety in one triangle becomes too high to be contained by it. Take any two points on your original triangle, identify a fourth party, and you've got a second triangle that shares one side with the first.

Chapter 5

I'm Okay; You're Dysfunctional

The One-Up One-Down Cha Cha

A t the end of Chapter 3, you were left wondering why Gwen, who is liked well enough by her own staff, is felt to be such a terror at the Pronto Agency. Motivated only by fear of her frequent explosions, the creative staff performs poorly on her account. It seems the more she checks up on them, the more they mess up. Let's take a closer look at how that situation evolved.

The first project Gwen brought to the agency was a direct-mail campaign aimed at boosting subscriptions to *Team Player Today*. Irv had rashly promised her that she could expect a 1 percent return rate on the campaign. When that didn't happen, Gwen held Pronto responsible and took her business to another agency. This led Irv to worry that he might lose the business of her parent company as well. Fortunately, a Pronto-designed campaign for *Hot Competition* was exceeding expectations, so Irv was able to remain in the good graces of Gwen's boss. When the second agency didn't have any better luck promoting *Team Player Today*, Gwen fired them as well. At that point, her boss insisted that she give Pronto another chance. It was the residue of anxiety left over from the earlier episode that led Irv to tell Susan that Gwen's account would be her "trial by fire."

As Susan reviewed the files on the account left by her predecessor, she spotted what she believed to be the reason the previous direct-mail campaign had failed. A focus group report had indicated that the name "Team Player

Today" left prospective subscribers cold. Susan decided that coming up with a new name should be the first order of business and set Rocky's staff to work on brainstorming suggestions. When Irv got wind of this, he told her to back off. He believed Gwen was personally attached to the current name and that any proposal that implied the failure of the previous campaign had anything to do with the magazine itself would offend her.

Susan had been hired in the first place partly because, according to her previous employer, she could really wow clients in presentations. But prevented by Irv from addressing what she knew to be the real problem, Susan lost confidence. Her first presentation to *Team Player Today* was lackluster. Gwen kept interrupting, throwing Susan off her rhythm. The admonishment not to say anything that might offend Gwen kept her from arguing when Gwen proposed bad ideas. The more Susan faded out, the more Gwen took over. By the end of the meeting, Gwen was at the white board, drafting a detailed outline of the site while Susan sat in bleak silence, taking notes.

"This won't work," Rocky said flatly, when Susan presented him with Gwen's outline. "The navigation structure is totally illogical. Visitors to the site are going to give up in frustration."

Steve had pretty much the same reaction. "Twenty sponsor ads on the home page? You've got to be kidding! Where are we supposed to put the content?"

"I know, I know," Susan said helplessly. "But what can I do? It's what the client wants. You'll just have to make it work somehow."

Rocky is not the sort of person who can be satisfied doing anything but his best work. The next day he presented Susan with a streamlined navigation scheme. "Look, show this to the client and see if she doesn't like it better," he urged.

"I can't," Susan said. "You don't understand what this client is like."

At that point Rocky decided to find out for himself what the client was like. He worked up a draft of the main-page copy done to Gwen's original specifications and emailed it to her along with his preferred version. His note began, "I've attached an alternative approach you might want to consider," and went on to outline the reasons why he thought it worked better. Gwen called him back right away to say that she liked some of his suggestions. Over the phone they hashed out points of disagreement and were able to come up with a compromise that Rocky found acceptable. He couldn't understand why Susan had been afraid to do it herself. Gwen was headstrong all right but not unwilling to listen to reason. You just had to know how to handle her.

Steve had less luck. The salespeople from *Team Player Today* had already promised twenty different advertisers an above-the-masthead spot on the home page, and it was now an inflexible design requirement. His strategy was simply to meet it and let Gwen see for herself how awful it looked. He figured this would be Susan's opportunity to renegotiate the specs. When Susan presented the design options Cheri had worked up, Gwen did indeed think they looked awful. "This won't do," she said. "You have to scroll for ages before you get to any editorial content."

"Maybe if we moved some of the ads to the bottom...." Susan said uncertainly.

"No can do," Gwen insisted. "They've got to be at the top. Tell the designers to make the masthead smaller and move the navigation buttons to the bottom of the page."

Susan made a careful note of this and passed the instruction on to Steve.

"Susan, if you make the masthead smaller than the ads, no one will be able to tell what site they're on," he protested.

"I know, I know," she sighed. "Do it anyway. The client is always right."

Cheri reduced the masthead, achieving the result Steve had predicted. Gwen hated it and insisted on yet another redesign, complaining at the same time that the project had by now fallen nearly a week behind schedule.

It was at this point that Gwen's staff decided to scrap *Team Player Today* and launch *My Way*. Rocky was charged with the task of writing press releases announcing the move. Now that he and Gwen had met, she was calling him directly instead of running her requests through

Susan. At first Rocky was content with this state of affairs, since he was better able than Susan to assert himself with Gwen. The trouble was that every time he sent her a new page of copy, she sent it back completely rewritten and three times as long. Her rambling, stuffy prose was about as readable as *Beowulf*. He would clean it up as best he could and send her the revised version only to have it sent back, rewritten once more and even worse. After several more rounds, Rocky decided to stop investing his own ego in the quality of the copy. Finding Gwen's revisions too painful to read, he just passed them on to the designers. As a result of his inattention, the press kit was sent out with several whopping grammatical errors. Maggie, the editor, spotted them right away and brought them to Gwen's attention. Gwen immediately called Susan in a rage. "Can't I trust you guys with anything?" she lamented. "From now on, I want to proofread everything before it's printed."

Earlier you heard Gwen say that she is not a micro-manager. Yet on this project, she has taken over the roles of copywriter, proofreader, designer, and project manager. She's on the phone to the agency twenty times a day, taking work home every night, and about to snap with nervous exhaustion. Why is she behaving this way?

If you put that question to Gwen, she would say, "If I don't do it, it won't get done right." She would support this with a list of their recent mistakes: missed deadlines, error-riddled copy, unattractive graphic design, and clumsy navigation. They, of course, would counter that all of these problems were arising from following Gwen's dumb orders.

It is her own anxiety that is causing Gwen to perceive the staff of Pronto as incompetent. She feels that the survival of her own organization depends on the success of the website. This pre-existing anxiety became heightened by the weak impression Susan made in their first meeting. To compensate for what she perceived to be Susan's lack of leadership, Gwen started *overfunctioning*—taking over Susan's job. Reluctant to assert her own role, Susan responded by *underfunctioning*.

From Susan's point of view, the causality works the other way around. She might agree that she is underfunctioning, but she would protest that it's because Gwen is overfunctioning. When she tries to do her job, Gwen takes over. She defers to Gwen because she believes she has no other choice. As she sees it, Gwen is a control freak.

Relationships of overfunctioning and underfunctioning are like that. You can never really tell who started doing it. You just find yourself in a vicious circle. The more the overfunctioner overdoes it, the more the underfunctioner underdoes it. And vice versa.

Gwen is not the only person who believes Susan is underfunctioning. Steve and Rocky think so too. It is the job of an account manager to maintain creative control, negotiate reasonable deadlines, dissuade the client from bad ideas, promote the creative staff's best thinking, and generally keep the client out of their hair. Susan isn't doing any of this. Whenever this particular client barks, Susan just rolls over and plays dead.

Because Susan's role is key to the success of the project, no one under her can function really well even if, like Steve, they are neither overfunctioning nor underfunctioning. As head designer, Steve's job is to execute to the best of his ability whatever specs he is given by the account manager. That's exactly what he does. But because the specs are dumb, the end result cannot help but be unsatisfactory. Getting the specs right is Susan's job. The more she underfunctions, the more anxious everyone else becomes.

Rocky's initial response is to overfunction. He takes over the job Susan isn't doing—tactfully persuading Gwen that her navigation scheme won't work. Gwen responds quite reasonably, for her own anxiety is eased by the fact that Rocky seems to know what he's doing and to be willing to take charge of the situation. She goes on relating to him directly because she finds his manner reassuring. But because she is by now locked into an overfunctioning mode, Gwen starts doing *his* job. Under pressure from Susan to accommodate the client no matter what, Rocky concludes that producing good copy just isn't worth the fight. Faced with Gwen's overfunctioning, he loses energy and starts to underfunction.

Not My Job

The terms "overfunctioning" and "underfunctioning" may seem to imply that for each person in an organization, there is some ideal or optimal level of functioning—neither too much nor too little. But what is it? When Gwen overfunctions, she believes that she needs to be doing what she's doing. She sees it as her responsibility. And when Susan underfunctions, she believes she can't or shouldn't do what she's not doing. So what's the objective standard? How do you tell what's really your responsibility and what isn't?

Your job description—and the other person's—should give you some pretty good clues. If what you're doing is part of someone else's job description and not your own, then you're probably overfunctioning. If you're not doing something that's in your job description, then you're probably underfunctioning.

Well, duh. Anyone could figure that out. So why is every workplace so full of over- and underfunctioners? By now you probably won't be surprised if I tell you that the root of the problem is anxiety. When people are anxious they both give and receive mixed messages about their own roles and their expectations of others. What's written on that job description, you probably haven't looked at since your first day of employment, seems pretty meaningless compared with the expectations of a co-worker who's right in your face, acting anxiously. Susan, for instance,

125

started off believing (correctly) that it was her job to figure out how to market her client's product more effectively. It was from her own boss that she got the message not
to do that part of her job. Instead, he led her to believe
that her task was to avoid saying anything that might
upset the client. Who could possibly succeed at such a
task? How Gwen might feel is something Susan can neither predict nor control. It's hardly any wonder that her
reaction to this impossible task was to stop talking altogether.

The principle that each person should do his or her
own job and no one else's tends to get muddled by the
rhetoric of teamwork that prevails in so many workplaces
today. To say, "That's not my job," or to insist that someone else stop butting in to what *is* your job is to risk the
accusation that you're "not a team player." But overfunctioning and underfunctioning actually have little to do
with the objective demands of anyone's job description.
They are styles of relating to *people*, not tasks.

When it comes to overfunctioning, the simple rule of
thumb is this: You are overfunctioning if what you are
doing puts you "one up" on the other person. Let's look at
some of the typical ways people do this in the workplace.

Worrying a lot about someone else.

Gerard is overfunctioning when he obsesses
about his staff losing confidence if sales don't pick
up. As head of the circulation department, it is his

I'm Okay; You're Dysfunctional

job to be concerned about the impact of poor sales on the company. It is up to him to provide the training, resources, and so forth that his staff needs in order to be successful. But it is not his job to provide them with self-esteem. Their mental health is their own business. Though you might say that he is a caring boss, what he is doing puts him in a one-up position. He is behaving as if his employees are his patients.

Thinking you know what's best for someone else.

We've seen Irv overfunction in this way on several occasions. He jumped to the conclusion that Gwen would be offended by Susan's proposal. Though Gwen had commissioned the market research on which it was based, he took it upon himself to decide that she would not wish to know the results. Because he prevented Susan from presenting the facts, Gwen never had a chance to make up her own mind about Susan's suggestion. He is taking a one-up position by placating her instead of letting her face the uncomfortable truth.

Giving advice before it's requested.

This is a way of making explicit that you think you know better than the other person what's good

127

for him or her. It implies that you think you're smarter. Irv gave both Susan and Steve unsolicited advice on how to get along with each other. Neither took it and both resented it.

Expecting others to do it your way.

As the client, Gwen is within her rights to state the objectives she expects the creative team at Pronto to meet for her. But she is overfunctioning when she starts taking over their jobs—writing the copy herself, telling the designers where to place the navigation buttons, and so forth. Gwen was also overfunctioning when she immediately presented her own staff with a solution, giving them no opportunity to explore other options. Overfunctioning is the common theme in her seemingly different anxiety reactions as manager and as client.

Taking over someone else's task without being asked.

Rocky was doing this when he negotiated with Gwen directly instead of leaving Susan to do it. Though she might justifiably have objected to this, Susan let it pass because the outcome was favorable and she was relieved she didn't have to do it herself. Nevertheless, Rocky created the impression in both their minds that he was better at doing Susan's job than Susan. He put himself in the one-up position. This came back to haunt him when he was no longer able to handle the client and Susan had totally given up on doing it herself.

Believing you are responsible for someone else's feelings.

Overfunctioners typically imagine that they have control over what others feel and what ought to make them feel better.

If you tend to overfunction in any of these ways, you are probably accustomed to thinking of it as "just being helpful." You might also be feeling under-appreciated, wondering why others aren't more grateful when you're constantly knocking yourself out on their behalf. Overfunctioners don't *intend* to put the other person down. The put-down is subtle and implicit, for taking over another's responsibility gives the impression that you don't think she can handle it herself.

Overfunctioning often sets up a chain reaction in which the other person begins to underfunction, leading the overfunctioning partner to feel all the more justified in continuing to take over. Susan slipped very quickly into the one-down role with both Irv and Gwen because she was new on the job and afraid of blowing the account. In her anxiety, she believed that she must take a submissive role to preserve her relationships with her boss and the client. She took this role so readily that both Irv and Gwen assumed it was what she really wanted.

Rocky initially resisted the one-down role by asserting himself. But when Gwen continued to overfunction, he resented the insult to his skills as a copywriter and sought to distance himself from his resentment by becoming less invested in the task. As a result of his withdrawal, he ended up underfunctioning after all.

It might not be obvious at first that when people overfunction, it's because they are anxious. Overfunctioners tend not to *feel* anxious. The one-up position makes them feel strong and in control. The underlying anxiety only begins to come to the surface when the overfunctioner makes a conscious effort to stop. Immediately he starts to imagine all the things that are likely to go wrong if he doesn't intervene. The knowledge that what others think, feel, and do is beyond his control is unsettling. Overfunctioners tend to believe that if a negative outcome they have anticipated does indeed come to pass, then it will be their own fault—even if preventing that outcome was someone else's job. They call this form of anxiety "having a sense of responsibility."

▼   ▼   ▼   ▼

To underfunction is to willingly take the "one-down" position. For underfunctioners, exercising their own power is what causes anxiety. They fear that they will be rejected if they stand up for themselves, and they are afraid of making mistakes. Let's look at some typical examples of underfunctioning at work.

Not making decisions.

Rather than commit to a course of action that might have bad results, the underfunctioner will put off making any decision at all. She waits for someone else to decide or simply lets events take their own course. If the underfunctioner is a manager, then subordinates will feel stymied, unclear about the boss's expectations, and unable to move forward with projects.

Constantly seeking advice.

Expressing one's own best thinking and then asking another for feedback is effective workplace behavior. To ask advice without first expressing your own thoughts is volunteering for the one-down position. The underfunctioner tends to just dump the problem or question into the lap of the nearest overfunctioner.

Habitually letting others have their way.

While we all have to compromise or accommodate sometimes to get along with others at work, underfunctioners give in without even mentioning their own needs and preferences. They are afraid they will be considered difficult if they say what they really think. The people who are being accommodated usually don't even realize there's a conflict.

Not taking initiatives.

Susan feels that emergencies and disasters are constantly just happening to her. Most of these negative outcomes are the result of her failing to alert the client or the creative staff to problems it is her job to foresee. Gwen is making all the decisions because Susan automatically gives in. But she is making *bad* decisions because Susan is failing to warn her of pitfalls and drawbacks.

Adopting a weak or helpless persona.

This is what Susan is doing when she tries to influence Steve with whining and wheedling. She hopes he will rescue her if she presents herself as a damsel in distress. With Gwen, she adopts a weak persona by taking the role of stenographer in a meeting where she could reasonably be expected to assume the lead. With Irv she behaves like a dutiful daughter, unconsciously accommodating his desire to take the paternal role.

Believing others are responsible for your feelings.

Underfunctioners typically imagine that they feel the way they feel because of what someone else is doing and that others ought to make them feel better.

These descriptions may be giving you the impression that underfunctioning and overfunctioning are personality traits. It is true that an individual may slip more readily into one or the other mode when anxious. Steve often finds himself coming to the rescue. Irv gives a lot of fatherly advice. Susan tends to fall into a passive role when she's nervous in a meeting. Gwen gets bossy.

Yet we have seen that when approached assertively, Gwen does not feel compelled to take a one-up position. Her behavior is influenced by that of others. At the first hint that the other person is underfunctioning, Gwen becomes anxious, and her response to anxiety is to over-function. If others manage their anxiety, then Gwen is able to manage hers. Most people are like Gwen in this respect. They take the one-down position if the other has claimed the one-up, or take the one-up position if the other is putting himself one-down. If you're caught up in such a relationship, forget trying to figure out who started it. The pattern has already begun to evolve before either party becomes conscious of it.

This is a handy thing to know if the poor perform-ance of someone in your organization is becoming a prob-lem for you. Typically, we look at the underfunctioner in isolation, label him or her as weak or incompetent, and focus on how to change this. Instead, look for the over-functioner. If one person is underfunctioning, there is probably an overfunctioner somewhere in the picture. It might be you.

This principle holds true of departments or teams as well as individuals. If one department is notably weak, then another is likely to be overfunctioning. Over at Gwen's magazine, everyone agreed that the circulation department was the weak link. So which department was overfunctioning? Those twenty sponsor ads above the masthead should give you a clue.

In response to declining subscriptions, the advertising sales department had for several years been attempting to pick up the slack. Their success in making up for lost subscriber revenue had made them the heroes of the team. Gwen rewarded them by boosting commission rates. This gave the sales people even greater incentive to perform. Since the bottom line wasn't growing despite increased ad sales, funds were moved from the editorial department budget to sales. Maggie had less money to pay writers and less space to put articles. The overall quality of the publication declined as it became cluttered with advertising. Gerard's department was not actually underfunctioning when they couldn't sell the thing. That readers no longer wanted the magazine was due to factors outside his control. One of those factors turned out to be the zeal of Tom's department. Instead of contributing to the success of the publication, their excessive productivity threw the ecology of the organization as a whole out of balance.

Sitting Out the Dance

So how do you stop overfunctioning or underfunctioning? In the real world, no one asks that question. The underfunctioner is more likely to ask, "How can I get my boss to stop micromanaging me?" The overfunctioner wonders how to get out from under the burden of doing another's job or worrying about another's problems. In the real world, we want to know how to change a relationship because we're getting fed up with the other person's behavior.

It isn't necessary to discuss the situation directly with your partner in the dance of one up and one down. The motive for such a talk would be to ask the other person to change—which only perpetuates the problem. Since the relationship is reciprocal, the other person will change his or her behavior in response to a change in yours. This doesn't need to be negotiated. It just happens.

The answer then to, "How can I get my boss to stop micromanaging?" is: stop underfunctioning. The answer to, "How can I get the underfunctioner to shape up?" is: stop overfunctioning.

The specifics of what you need to start doing if you are an underfunctioner, or stop doing if you are an over-functioner, will vary. They're not hard to figure out. The obstacle to changing is not that you don't know what to do but rather coping with the anxiety that comes up the moment you even consider it. So let me offer some thoughts that might help with that.

If You Tend to Overfunction...

You probably worry that if you stop taking over for the underfunctioner, then she will fail. This is possible but perhaps not as likely as you think. Underfunctioning is a way of relating to others and has very little to do with objective competence. It is rare that an underfunctioner, thrown back on her own resources, turns out to be truly incapable. Presenting herself as ineffectual and weak is more usually a relationship pattern that will change soon after her partner in the dance stops overfunctioning.

Nevertheless, breaking the pattern does mean learning to live with a certain loss of control. Maybe the underfunctioner *will* fail if you stop bailing her out. That this is not your fault and not something you ought to prevent is an idea that takes getting used to.

It can be especially hard to stop overfunctioning if the underfunctioner is your subordinate. You can then make a pretty good argument that her performance *is* your responsibility. In that case, you will need to separate the facts about your responsibility from the *feeling* of being responsible. It might help to make a list of things supervisors can legitimately be expected to do—in other words, the facts about your job. Your list might include:

▶ Stating clear and attainable performance expectations

▶ Giving clear and objective feedback on performance

▶ Providing the tools, resources, and information needed to do the job

▶ Delegating the authority needed to do the job.

It might also include such emotion-laden items as "building the employee's self-esteem" or "ensuring appropriate work/life balance." Ask yourself whether it is within your power to do these things. Sure, it's within your power to refrain from calling someone an idiot (and by all means do refrain), but can you really control how she feels about herself? Can you control how she feels about *you*? How she feels about the job? The answers to all these questions is NO. This person is your subordinate, not your patient.

When you are tempted to say to yourself, "I feel responsible," try substituting, "I feel anxious." This might not sound right at first. But the first time you deliberately refrain from overfunctioning, you will notice that you are indeed anxious. You have actually been anxious all along but were too busy before to notice. If you feel you must come to someone's rescue, then come to your own. Give yourself some advice on how to cope with your anxiety.

If You Tend to Underfunction...

Unlike the overfunctioner, you probably already realize you're anxious. You are at some level afraid of what will happen if you assert yourself; otherwise you wouldn't be accepting the one-down position. The way past this anxiety is to focus on the power you already have in the relationship. Imagine for a moment that everything happening with the overfunctioner has been happening at *your* initiative. (I know it doesn't feel like that, but pretend.) Each time the other person over-functions, it is in response to some cue you have given him or her. What was that cue? It may be something as simple as raising the pitch of your voice at the end of a statement, as if it were a question. Once you see that you are already affecting the relationship with these cues, it is a fairly simple matter to change them. The key is to realize that you've never been as helpless as you are feeling.

You get out of a one-down position by taking an I-position. This means deciding and communicating what you really think—not about the other person but about the issue or problem at hand. An I-position is a forthright statement of what you believe, know, or intend to do. It ends with a period, not a question mark.

Sometimes people underfunction when they feel they're in a no-win situation. For example, it may seem that you're being given mixed messages about what is wanted or asked to meet contradictory expectations. That is Susan's predicament. Resolving it, as she has so far, by not taking firm action in *any* direction is underfunction-ing. Paralyzed by fear that she will displease somebody, she ends up displeasing everybody. Steve, faced with the same predicament, resolves it by taking an I-position. Knowing that he can't please everyone, he decides what *he* wants to do. Life is an endless series of no-win situations if what you mean by winning is making everyone else happy.

When one person in a one-up/one-down relationship changes his or her behavior, the other person may push back at first. Pushback is resistance to change, for even a change for the better in an unsatisfactory relationship arouses anxiety. The underfunctioner may act more helplessly than ever. The overfunctioner may become even more overbearing. This may tempt you to conclude that the relationship can't be altered no matter what you do. If you are thinking this, it is because you are focused on the other person's behavior, which you do not have the power to change. But no one can stop *you* from changing. Because it is reciprocal, a one-up/one-down relationship cannot continue indefinitely if you're not playing your part. Eventually the other person will either change his or her own behavior or else find another partner.

In Summary...

 Overfunctioning and underfunctioning are ways of relating to people, not tasks. In assuming the one-up position, the overfunctioner feels strong and in control. In assuming the one-down position, the underfunctioner avoids the perceived relationship losses that might come of self-assertion. Both overfunctioning and underfunctioning are reactions to anxiety. The overfunctioner takes the one-up position in order to feel strong and in control. The underfunctioner takes the one-down position in order to avoid self-assertion.

Examples of overfunctioning include: giving unsolicited advice, worrying excessively about someone else, thinking you know what's best for someone else, micromanaging, and believing you are responsible for someone else's feelings.

 Examples of underfunctioning include: avoiding decisions, not taking initiatives, constantly seeking advice, adopting a weak or helpless persona, and believing that others are responsible for your feelings.

 Overfunctioning/underfunctioning is a reciprocal relationship in which each person's behavior prompts and seems to justify the other's. Because these are *relationship* behaviors, neither can exist without the other. If someone is overfunctioning, then someone else is probably underfunctioning, and vice versa.

 Either partner in a one-up/one-down relationship can stop the cycle by changing her own behavior. While the other person may initially push back, he will eventually respond either by changing his behavior as well or by finding a different partner.

Chapter 6

Nothing Personal

Blame, cutoff, and open warfare

"Would you believe this is my third head cold in as many months?" Susan said to me as she tossed another spent tissue into the wastebasket beside her chair. "Stress-related, I'm sure. This is the most dysfunctional company I've ever worked for."

Having tuned in to five previous episodes of the Pronto soap opera, you may be tempted by now to agree with Susan's assessment of it. Dysfunctional—a polite way of saying "screwed up"—is the term most often applied these days to organizations where conflict runs high.

It's not a term I use. Wherever two or more are gathered, conflict is natural and inevitable. You might even be getting the impression by now that I'm downright in favor of it. In Chapter 3, you saw how suppression of differences in pursuit of a quixotic ideal of group harmony inhibited the *Team Player* team from facing and resolving the dilemma of a declining customer base. Conflict avoidance and the behaviors it spawns—conformity, groupthink, overemphasis on making everyone feel good—are every bit as threatening to the survival of an organization as open feuds and turf wars. An organization thrives only to the extent that its members are fully and intelligently engaged. When individuals really care about what they're doing, have strong convictions about it, it is natural for them to clash. Healthy conflict—by which I mean conflict in which the participants manage themselves well—can be the creative lifeblood of an organization. Handled well, conflict is highly functional. What is potentially harmful to an organization is *mismanaged* conflict.

At the time Susan came to see me, she was feeling increasingly isolated. Despite the urgency of the *My Way* project, she found herself putting off action until the last possible moment, inflicting needless emergencies on the creative staff. Their resentment of the stress she was causing them intensified to the point where they could barely remain civil. This caused her to dread contact with them even more, leading to further procrastination, emergencies, and frayed tempers. Cheri was now refusing to take last-minute assignments that hadn't been cleared through Steve. Jennifer was giving her the cold shoulder, and the other account execs also kept their distance, as if her incompetence were some contagion they were afraid of catching. She felt like a pariah. As the feeling of being rejected by her co-workers grew, she began to avoid the office. She attempted to relieve her stress with long midday workouts at the gym and often arrived late on the mornings after sleepless nights. She was thinking seriously of resigning—that is, if she wasn't fired first.

As our previous analyses of the situation at Pronto should by now have demonstrated, Susan was not the sole cause of the conflicts there. Nevertheless, she was becoming the first person everyone else looked to blame. The more they blamed, the more evidence she seemed to present that she was blameworthy.

What do we mean when we use the word "blame" as a noun? Like the proverbial hot potato, no one wants to be left holding it. But what *is* it? Ever stop to wonder that?

You might start by saying that to blame (the verb) is to attribute responsibility for some problem or mishap to the one who caused it. For example, if there are errors in printed copy and it is Rocky's job to proofread the copy, then Rocky is, in principle, "to blame." Yet it is unlikely that anyone will invest much energy in blaming him. As soon as he says, "Sorry, my mistake," everyone is likely to shrug and think no more of it. Blame as a noun, a thing, seems to exist as long as everyone is trying to pass it around but tends to disappear the moment it is accepted.

Yet there are other mishaps around that everyone is quite keen to avoid taking blame for. All concerned would rather catch bubonic plague than say, "Sorry, my mistake." Obviously there is more to blame than the objective assignment of responsibility. In fact, the clearer it is who is responsible for a mishap, the less anyone cares about blame. Groups are most preoccupied with blame in situations where the objective cause of the problem is difficult to pinpoint.

From the standpoint of relationship-systems theory, blame is the acute focus of a group's chronic anxiety. When a systemic problem is going round in vicious triangles, those affected tend to believe that their pain can be relieved by identifying who started it. They all know that *they* weren't the one who started it. By now you're probably coming to understand that no one else did either. Systemic problems co-evolve and have no clear starting point. Blame is the arbitrary identification of one individual or event as the cause of undesirable subsequent events. To be blamed is to become a casualty of faulty causality.

This is obviously unfortunate for the person who is the object of blame. What may be less obvious is that it is likewise unfortunate for those doing the blaming. To blame is to declare oneself powerless while at the same time exaggerating the power of the one who is blamed. Yet that person rarely *feels* powerful, for if she is the one left holding the hot potato, it is because she is the one least capable of getting rid of it. The net result of blame is that *no one* feels powerful, for control is being attributed to the most helpless actor in the situation.

In organizations where anxiety is often expressed in blame, to avoid being blamed becomes a constant preoccupation. People attempt to preempt blame by sending each other memos recapitulating who did what and when. Their attention shifts from avoiding a potential problem to avoiding *being blamed* for it. That's why Susan takes so many notes in her meetings with Gwen. She rarely refers to her own notes or makes any practical use of them. Instead, she types them up and sends them to Gwen. Though she would say that she is attempting to avoid later misunderstandings, she is actually establishing evidence that if a misunderstanding does occur, it was not her fault. What this behavior subtly communicates to Gwen is that

Susan anticipates trouble. Gwen starts anticipating it too. Susan's expectation of being blamed becomes self-fulfilling.

Scapegoating is a variation on blame in which a single individual becomes the sole focus of a group's anxiety. That person comes to be thought of as The Problem itself rather than just the cause of a specific mishap. The usual scapegoat is the group's most reactive member. By that, I mean the one who feels the collective anxiety most acutely and acts it out most conspicuously. Susan's reactions—underfunctioning, being pushed to the outside position in every triangle she creates, unwelcome pursuit, and untimely distancing—are annoying to others. Yet it is not annoyance alone that leads them to scapegoat her. The obviousness of Susan's anxiety itself makes those around her uncomfortable. It brings to the foreground the chronic anxiety the rest of them are usually able to ignore. Rather than own the anxiety they themselves are feeling, they concentrate on Susan's. The more they see her as a "case," the less they feel their own anxiety. Susan's evident weakness makes them feel stronger.

As one member of the group assumes the scapegoat position, the others distance themselves. It's as if the weak member has cooties. The more they are reluctant to talk *to* her, the more they tend to talk *about* her. They form triangles with each other in which the scapegoat is put in the outside position. By triangling, they feel greater solidarity with each other, which further reduces their own anxiety

and awareness of their own responsibility. Increasingly isolated, the scapegoat may find at least one ally in an overfunctioner. That person's response to anxiety is to attempt
to protect and/or rehabilitate the scapegoat. This is the
role Irv has adopted with Susan. Because he's the CEO,
she's not in immediate danger of being fired. That her
incompetence is not being punished only increases the
others' resentment of her. While she still technically *has*
her job, she becomes less and less able to *do* it.

The Canary in the Mineshaft

A few days after our most recent meeting, Steve
called me to say, "Maybe I won't need to confront Irv after all. I have the feeling Susan's on
her way out. My troubles may soon be over."

"How do you figure that?" I asked.

"That Susan's leaving? Well—"

"No, I mean how do you figure her leaving means
your troubles are over?"

"You're kidding, right? Susan's been the major thorn
in my side all along. And I'm not the only one she's driving nuts."

"So all will be well if she leaves."

"All will be tolerable, anyhow."

"That's too bad. Tolerable anxiety tends not to be
addressed."

"Maybe so. But what's so bad about that? I could tolerate a little tolerable anxiety just fine right now."

"Steve, in an anxious organization, there's always a Susan. Think of her as the canary in the mineshaft. If one canary dies, then another takes her place. Might be Susan's successor. Might be someone else in the company. But, for sure, there's going to be another canary. So the question is, how many canaries have to die before you decide the tolerable anxiety isn't so tolerable after all?"

"You've lost me. Why is there always a canary?"

When scapegoating occurs, it is as if the chronic anxiety that had been spread throughout the system now comes to rest on the shoulders of a single individual. The group is able to deny that its anxiety is shared and systemic. A collective myth develops: that all had been well before the problem person became such a problem. Its corollary is that all will be well once the problem person is gotten rid of.

In a tense relationship, temporary distancing can be quite helpful. It allows you to cool off and get some perspective on the situation. But as an unconscious anxiety reaction, distancing can lead to trouble. In Susan's case, it is taking the form of procrastination—distancing from difficult relationships at moments when engagement is essential.

Sometimes distance comes as such a relief that one or both parties are tempted to make it permanent, to cut off relationships altogether. In the workplace, it is rarely possible to sever all contact, yet it does sometimes happen that a person is, for all intents and purposes, cut off. Individuals do sometimes find themselves left permanently out of the loop. In a large organization the cutoff member may be "kicked upstairs"—perhaps given an important-sounding but meaningless title and no significant responsibilities. In a family-owned business, a family member may hold a title yet rarely show up at work. Individuals may also cut themselves off, going through the motions of their job while ceasing to be a "player." A small company like Pronto can rarely afford to employ dead wood, particularly in a position as crucial as account executive. For Susan, cutoff can only mean resigning or getting fired.

As Susan has not been performing well, her departure might not seem like any great loss. But by now it should be clear to you that her lackluster performance has been precipitated by factors that will not disappear if she disappears. Blaming one person for a systemic problem allows everyone to ignore the fact that the problem *is* systemic. They partake of the illusion that in assigning blame, they have identified the source of the problem and even gone halfway to solving it. Once a scapegoat has been found, all further thinking about the situation is suspended. If the scapegoat is pushed out, then the group cuts off not only from the individual but also from the underlying issues.

Earlier Steve had recognized that one aspect of the systemic problem was ambiguous messages from the CEO. Irv has been treating the conflict between Susan and

Steve as a personality clash instead of acknowledging and taking a stand on the issue involved. The need to confront this matter with Irv raises anxiety for Steve. While he is hesitating, the collective move to scapegoat Susan seems to present him with a reprieve. The issue with Irv suddenly doesn't seem so important after all. Irv is off the hook too. He can focus on what to do about Susan and remain oblivious to his own impact on the system. Nobody is thinking that Irv has anything to do with creating this problem. Get rid of Susan and the problem will re-emerge in a new form while all concerned continue to be clueless as to its source.

To return to Steve's question: why is there always a dying canary? The chronic anxiety in the mineshaft is why. Canaries will keep dying until you air out the mineshaft—that is, address the systemic source of the anxiety. Irv's well-meaning mixed messages will continue to put staff members in conflict with one another until his position is clarified. Gwen's behavior will continue to put stress on the writers and designers until an account manager takes proper charge of the situation. No account manager is likely to do that so long as Irv's directive is to pacify the client at all costs. If Susan is cut off at this point, it is unlikely that these issues will ever be addressed. Once an anxious organization resorts to "human sacrifice," chronic anxiety increases as the survivors secretly fear that their turn is coming. Further resignations and dismissals are likely to ensue. In organizations with high employee turnover, cutting off from issues has left cutting off from individuals the only solution to conflict that anyone can think of.

Getting to the Root of Conflict

Steve must have taken my lecture to heart, for he dropped out of the growing movement to scapegoat Susan. As a conciliatory gesture, he told her about his work with me and suggested that she give me a call. That's how she and her packet of tissues come to be sitting across from me in my office. "Maybe you can help us communicate better," she said. "If Steve and I could just confront our differences, I'm sure we could work it out. But I don't know how to get him to see my side. I don't feel like he's really open to my point of view."

"So, as you see it, these conflicts you're involved in are what's making you anxious," I offer, when she pauses to blow her nose again.

She shoots me a withering look. "Tell me something I don't already know."

"Okay. What you don't already know is that it's the other way around. You are having conflicts because you are anxious."

"You mean my anxiety is causing the conflict? I don't see that. I mean, sure, when I'm stressed maybe I'm not so effective at managing other people, maybe I'd do better at that if I could calm down....But Steve has been resisting me from day one. He just plain doesn't want to do what I want him to do. That's the objective problem."

"In other words, you and Steve disagree."

"Obviously. We have a conflict."

"Try looking at it a different way. You have conflict because you are *anxious* about the disagreement."

"Same difference. What you're saying is just semantics."

"So you disagree with what I'm saying."

Susan nods.

"Would you call what's happening at this moment a conflict?"

"Not really, no. It's just a friendly disagreement. There's nothing upsetting about it."

"Why not?"

"Because there's not much at stake. But with Steve, there's a lot at stake. If I can't get him to come on board, then we may lose the *My Way* account. And my head's the one that's going to roll if we do."

"So naturally you are anxious."

Susan smiles wryly. "Walked right into that one, didn't I?"

"You experience the disagreement as a conflict because you are anxious about the outcome."

"Touché. But it still sounds like a distinction without a difference. What's your point?"

"What if I were to tell you that what you need to manage in this situation is not Steve but your own anxiety?"

"That doesn't help me. What I keep trying to get you to see is there's an objective problem here. Anyone in my position would be anxious."

"Perhaps. As I understand it, Steve has been taking the same position on timeframes with all of the account executives. In your observation, are they all feeling as upset about it as you are?"

Susan groans. "That's just it! They damn well ought to be. We should all be sticking together on this issue, but Jennifer seems to have gone over to Steve's side. Even when he blew her deadline, she didn't make an issue of it. I think she figures if she makes nice with him, he'll give her better service. So I'm stuck being the heavy."

"Would it be fair then to say that you're feeling an anxiety about Steve's position that Jennifer doesn't seem to be feeling?"

"Evidently. Yeah. I guess Jennifer can sleep at night if she misses a client deadline. Not all of us can."

"Why is that?"

Susan shrugs. "Different work ethic, I suppose. I've always been the A student."

"What happens if you get a B?"

"B is the same as F where I come from."

"Your family, you mean."

"My dad. Yeah."

"He expected you to be brilliant at every subject?"

She rolls her eyes. "I wouldn't say that. He just expected me to get good grades."

"Sorry, I don't follow."

"His favorite saying was, 'Don't be smart.' We used to argue a lot at the dinner table—over politics and such—and any time I scored a point, he'd say that. 'Don't be smart.' In other words, get straight A's but don't actually think for yourself." She plucks another tissue from the packet in her lap. "How'd we get into my dad? I hope you're not going to tell me it's just my inner child that wants Steve to meet deadlines. I mean, please."

"No. That may be a perfectly valid position for you to be taking on this issue. But the emotional intensity you're feeling is probably being triggered by anxiety you felt in the past. You feel that if you can't get Steve to do it your way, then it will be a personal failure on your part. You'll be bringing home a bad report card. And that puts you in a bind, because you can't control what Steve does. So you feel anxious."

"I can't control what *anyone* does around here. But I'm supposed to. That's what you're not getting. I'm supposed to meet all these crazy demands from the client, and I'm supposed to do it without driving the creative staff crazy. It's impossible!"

"That's true," I say calmly. "And you can't possibly succeed at doing the impossible, can you?"

"Believe me, I'm trying."

"That would tend to explain why you're so worn out."

"Tell me about it!"

"Are further attempts to do the impossible likely to meet with success?"

"No," Susan admits. "But what else can I do?"

"That's what we're here to figure out."

Our dialogue did not proceed very efficiently from there, for Susan's anxiety was so high that she could not think clearly. I'll fast forward past the many relapses into self-blame, self-pity, and blame of others to the part where we began to make real headway.

I said, "You mentioned earlier that your father expected you to get straight A's and at the same time kept telling you not to be smart. That sounds like quite a bind. Does the situation you're in at Pronto feel like the same kind of bind?"

"You mean: be smart/don't be smart?"

I nod.

"Save the client's sinking magazine, but don't ever talk about why it's sinking. There's a bind for you."

"Where did that one come from?"

"Irv. But surely you're not suggesting that *Irv's* the one to blame for my troubles. He's the one person around here who seems to be on my side."

"Blame. My side. That's emotion talking again, Susan."

"Sorry. I still don't get it."

"When we're coming from anxiety, we see conflict in terms of personalities—who's nice and who's mean, who's for us and who's against us. On an emotional level, you feel comfortable with Irv. He's nice to you. Steve is not so nice to you. Your relationship is adversarial. Steve must therefore be your problem and Irv, your ally."

"Well, yeah, obviously."

"Try detaching from that for a moment. If you can set aside how you feel about the personalities involved and look instead at the issues—"

"Then my real problem is Irv. Is that what you're saying?"

"Not quite. Getting warmer, though. Think *issues*."

"Okay. The *issue* is what Irv has been asking me to do. Manage this crucial project without taking a stand about anything. Don't think. Because if I say what I think, I might upset the client. Be smart, don't be smart, in other words."

"Precisely. If you try to manage a project without asserting yourself—"

"I can't"

"Right. And how does that affect Steve and Rocky?"

"The client drives them round the bend, and they think I'm supposed to do something about that."

"Is that a reasonable expectation for them to have?"

"Not if I can't ever put my foot down with a client. According to Irv, if the client wants it yesterday, we turn back time. So it's my job to tell Steve to turn back time."

"Which would you rather do—say No to the client or demand that Steve deliver what she wants?"

"To tell you the truth, I don't really care. I could go either way. What's impossible is going *neither* way, and that's what Irv is asking of me. I can accommodate Gwen or I can accommodate Steve, but I can't do both. Irv needs to see that."

"And what would make him see it?"

"I don't know. Maybe...I could tell him?"

"Sounds like a plan to me."

"Wow. All this time I've been thinking I have this huge conflict with Steve and this other huge conflict with Gwen. But it's really *their* needs that are in conflict, and...well, it's nothing personal, is it?"

Your Adversary Is Not Your Enemy

With that last statement, Susan has grasped the essence of the matter: conflict is nothing personal. This is difficult to see, for when a relationship becomes adversarial, when we are angry with a co-worker or he or she seems angry with us, it sure *feels* personal. Like Susan, many people go on to assume that the solution is better communication. "If we could just confront our differences, understand each other better...." But communication—whether in the form of a confrontational showdown or a gentle heart-to-heart talk—rarely solves the problem. That is because the conflict is not really between the two people who seem to be having it. Their relationship is simply the point in the system where anxiety happened to erupt.

The anxiety around which Susan and Steve have erupted is caused by a lack of clarity in the organization as a whole around two issues: how the demands of clients and the needs of employees are to be balanced, and the role of the account executive. Imagine that before an ad agency opened for business, a group of "founding fathers" were to get together to draft a constitution for it. They would debate these issues in the abstract, attempting to determine the wisest policies. While the debate might be vigorous, it would probably not engender anxiety. But now that the agency is in business, the lack of clear policies has led to mishaps for which the employees are inclined to blame each other. These incidents, rather than the underlying issues, become the focus of everyone's attention, and a source of anxiety. What at a constitutional convention would have been a debate has, in the workplace, become a conflict. To put it another way, ambiguity in the rational system of the organization is being experienced as an upset in the emotional system.

At the root of most workplace conflicts is an impersonal issue—an ambiguity in the rational system. It may be about the organization's mission, how it is to go about achieving that mission, the relative importance of various goals and values, the allocation of resources, or the definition of job roles. When these matters are left undefined or contradictory messages about them are being sent, individual members will likely make differing assumptions, jump to differing conclusions, or push for differing agendas. The resulting disagreements are healthy for an organization when they bring the underlying issues into focus. In the course of settling these disagreements, the organization better defines itself.

Before conflict can be productive of such clarity, however, the participants have to calm down. The underlying issues cannot emerge if people are taking the conflict personally—that is, believing it is about their relationship to another person. Even now, you may be finding this difficult to see. Thinking of a particular conflict you have with someone at work, the feature you find most striking may be that person's obnoxious behavior toward you. Susan sees Steve's bullheaded refusal to give in to her demands. Steve sees Susan's shrill outbursts and constant attempts to manipulate the situation by triangling. To be able to identify the underlying issue, you need to get factual and neutral about the interpersonal unpleasantness that has arisen from it.

How the other person is behaving is simply his reaction to anxiety. It may be triggered by factors outside of your relationship with him, such as how he reacted to similar situations in childhood. It might also be provoked by whatever it is *you* do in reaction to anxiety. Steve shuts down when Susan is shrill; Susan gets shrill when Steve shuts down. Because in their respective anxiety reactions they keep rubbing each other the wrong way, they come to believe that they are adversaries, that they are in conflict with each other. They are not. They have a mutual problem in the lack of clarity about a certain issue and a mutual interest in solving it. They are, in a sense, the two insiders in a triangle with the issue itself. How this insight can be used to approach issues constructively is a topic we'll tackle in the next chapter.

In Summary...

 Conflict is natural and inevitable. Whether it hurts or helps an organization depends on how it is handled.

 The perception of conflict arises when disagreement over an issue raises anxiety. It is the anxiety, not the disagreement, that causes conflict.

 Just because a person is acting adversarial doesn't mean he or she is your adversary. The true source of your conflict may be an impersonal issue about which you both have a mutual interest in achieving clarity.

 Blaming and attempting to avoid blame are expressions of anxiety that arise when the cause of a problem or mishap is ambiguous. In the absence of anxiety, problems are simply corrected without assigning blame. Preoccupation with blame is a sign that a systemic problem in the organization is not being identified and addressed.

 In scapegoating, the chronic anxiety of a group becomes concentrated on a single individual. The scapegoat is generally the most reactive person in the group—that is, the one who feels the anxiety most acutely and acts it out most obviously. Focusing on the scapegoat distracts the other group members from their own anxiety and makes them feel stronger.

 Temporary distancing may be helpful in taking the heat out of conflict. Complete severance of a difficult relationship—i.e., cutoff—seldom occurs in the workplace without a dismissal or resignation. Dealing with a conflict in this way usually leads to cutting off from the underlying issue as well as the person. In that case, the conflict will reemerge elsewhere in the organization.

 High employee turnover is often a sign that cutoff has become the preferred or only method of dealing with acute anxiety in an organization.

Chapter 7

Getting a Grip

How to stay calm, clear, and
collected in a crazy system

"**I**'ve had a brainstorm," Susan announced to me over the phone, about a week after our first meeting.

"Tell me."

"Well, remember how I'd decided I needed to ask Irv to clarify his expectations? I'm thinking now it might not be necessary. See, I was all wound up because I thought he expected me to keep everybody happy. But then it dawned on me that I haven't kept *anyone* happy. I mean, worst-case scenario, right? Only here's the thing—I haven't kept everyone happy, *and I haven't been fired.* It suddenly occurred to me that all this fear I've been feeling is coming from me, not from Irv. I mean, sure, he wants everyone happy. Who wouldn't? But what's been keeping me up nights is *my* anxiety, not Irv's."

"That's some brainstorm all right," I agreed. "Congratulations."

She laughed. "I slept nine hours last night. Can you believe it? But listen, I haven't even gotten to the good part yet. I figured since the client is upset with me all the time, I'm obviously no good at not upsetting her. So instead of worrying about that, I decided to just start telling her what I really think. I mean, she's already fed up with me, so what do I have to lose?"

"Have you tried it yet?"

"Yes! And you're not going to believe it—"

"Try me."

"Well, we're in one of those meetings where she's marking up web pages and trashing up the design with all her changes. You know, micromanaging. Usually I just write down all of her demands and pass them along to Steve. But this time I explained the rationale behind Cheri's design. I went into all the options she and Steve had considered and why the choices they had made were the best choices."

"How did Gwen react?"

"Amazingly well! That's what I can't get over. Instead of continuing to push her own solutions, she told me what her concerns were. She was very calm about it. I told her I would convey her concerns to the designers and that I was confident they would find good solutions. Not only did she accept that, but when we sent her some additional pages later in the week, her only comment was, 'Great. Keep up the good work.'"

"I imagine that came as a relief to Steve and Cheri."

"Relief is not the word. Steve looked like he was about to drop dead of amazement. He was really pleased. Isn't that ironic? I actually did manage to please both sides but only when I stopped trying to."

"How would you explain that?"

"Maybe Gwen just needed to hear that I had confidence in the designers. When I told her the reasons for their choices, I suppose it reassured her that we weren't just shooting from the hip. She could feel her project was in good hands."

"So she got calm when you got calm."

"Yeah. You know what else? I'm thinking now that what Steve has been saying about deadlines is not so unreasonable. It freaked me out at first because it meant I'd have to take a stand with clients—and I'm still not sure Irv really supports that. Sometimes the clients really do insist on tight timeframes, and sometimes they have a good reason. It may be unavoidable. But I've been giving in without even stating what a reasonable timeframe would be. I always say, 'When do you want it?' and the answer is always 'Yesterday.' I could start instead by taking a position. Like, 'We can have it to you in a week.' At least I wouldn't be *volunteering* to make everyone stay late."

"What will you do if the client says a week is too long to wait?"

"I'm still not sure about that. I think that's going to have to be Irv's call."

"So you still do need some clarification from him."

"Yes. Possibly. But it feels different. When I imagined doing it before, I sounded so whiny. Like, 'You want me to make everyone happy, and I can't.' Poor little me. Now it's more like, 'Okay, what's our company's policy on this thing?' Do you see what I mean?"

"It's about issues rather than feelings."

"Precisely."

Broaching the Real Issue

The following week, it was Steve who called me. "Wait till you hear the latest! I'd set up an appointment to talk to Irv Monday afternoon. But that morning, at our management staff meeting, someone else beat me to it. And you'll never guess who. Susan!" He went on to give me a rundown of what had occurred at the meeting. It went something like this.

Susan began, addressing Irv. "You've asked us to support the policy Steve has set up around timeframes, and I agree it's a good policy from the employee-friendliness standpoint. What isn't clear to me is what we account execs are supposed to do if the client insists on a faster turnaround."

Irv said, "As I understand it, Steve is willing to be flexible in those cases. Isn't that right, Steve?"

"Sure. Well, I suppose it depends on what you mean by flexible. When our workload is fairly light, we may be able to accommodate a faster timeframe without disrupting staff schedules. But what happens when we can't? My position has been that we ought to tell the client No in those cases."

"And that's the part I'm unclear about," Susan said. "Do we support Steve's policy if it means saying No to a client?"

"I think we can take that on a case-by-case basis," said Irv.

"I'm not really comfortable with that," said Steve. "It means that in some cases I will have to make last-minute overtime demands on the designers. Kind of defeats the whole principle of setting up predictable work schedules."

"Yes," Susan agreed. "And also, who makes the decision? Is Steve supposed to make the exception on the say-so of the account exec? And if so, on what basis do we decide that our client warrants an exception. I mean, I *always* think my own client should be the exception," Susan concluded with a self-deprecating laugh.

Steve laughed too. "Tell me about it!"

"Well, I have to admit, you guys are putting me on the spot," Irv said. "I hadn't given this a lot of thought. In principle, the creative team takes their marching orders from the account execs because it's the execs who are in the best position to judge client needs. So, yes, if you agree to a shorter timeframe, I would expect Steve to go along. But I would also hope that you'd use good judgment in making that request, that you'd take Steve's scheduling needs into account."

"In other words, we're supposed to weigh the client's needs against the needs of staff?"

"Yes, that's right. That's exactly right."

"What I'm asking, though, is *how* do we weigh it? By who's going to be the most upset?"

"The squeaky wheel always gets the grease," Jennifer put in. "Doesn't seem quite fair somehow. Doesn't that just encourage all the wheels to get squeakier?"

"Well, the ultimate goal is client satisfaction" Irv said. "The timeframes Steve has set up are pretty reasonable, and I'd like you to make your best effort to conform to them. Ultimately, though, if the client wants it faster, then we give it to them faster. Quick turnaround is one of our distinguishing features as an agency. It's what we're known for. Again and again, clients mention it as a factor in their choosing us over other agencies. That's how we've positioned ourselves in the market, and it has worked for the last decade."

"So, bottom line, if I tell Steve the client wants it faster, then he has to do it faster. Is that right?"

"Right."

"Okay, that's clearer. Only there's one part that still has me confused. Is it part of my job to persuade the client not to want it faster? I have the impression that's what Steve is expecting me to do. Am I right Steve?"

"Truthfully? Yeah. Sometimes. I think if you were more assertive, you could get the client to flex a little."

"You see the problem?" Susan said to Irv. "It becomes a matter of personalities. Steve is probably right about my needing to me more assertive at times. I'm sure he's right about that. But if we are positioned as a quick-turnaround agency, it shouldn't be up to me to talk clients out of wanting quick turnaround."

"I have to admit Susan has a point," Steve conceded.

"I don't expect you to talk clients out of what they want," said Irv. "Satisfying the client is your job, and I trust you to know how best to do it. It's your call, Susan."

"Well, at least he was clear," Steve said to me. "Wasn't what I wanted to hear, but it couldn't have been clearer. In a funny way I was relieved. It took the pressure off my relationship with Susan. I saw that it wasn't really her fault my policy wasn't working. What I'm trying to do just isn't congruent with the goals of the agency. I didn't realize that before because Irv had never stated the goals so plainly."

"So where does that leave you?"

"Well, by now I have become so invested in my policy that I wanted to give it at least one last shot. So in my private meeting with Irv that afternoon, I made my case for it. But I took a different approach than I had in the past. You see, behind this position I've been taking is a vision of what our agency could be. It seems to me that clients are willing to wait for top-of-the-line design—or top-of-the-line anything. To emphasize speed is to de-emphasize quality. Almost like damning by faint praise. If our position were, 'Great design doesn't happen overnight,' and we really delivered on quality, I believe we'd attract a class of clients who were not only less antsy but also willing to pay more. We've got staff talented enough to deliver that quality right now. They've never been able to perform at the level they're capable of because they're always under such time pressure."

"What was Irv's response to that?"

"He heard me out. He agreed completely that an agency could be successful with that strategy. Even said that maybe one day I'd start one of my own, that he could see me making a go of it. But it's not the strategy he wants for Pronto. This quick-turnaround thing has worked well for him, and he wants to stick with it."

"That must have been a disappointment for you."

"You'd think so. Oddly enough, I felt okay about it. It helps to know where he stands. And I'd never have found out if I hadn't told him where *I* stand. So I don't consider this I-position of mine à failure. But I see that my policy isn't going to work. We spent the rest of the meeting talking about that."

"Tell me more."

"Well, as I said before, if fast service is our market position, then my operation has to support that. I've been recruiting staff on the basis of my own vision of quality. To achieve Pronto's goals, I'm going to have to give more weight than I have been to a candidate's availability to work weird hours. Rocky has less trouble than I do with the turnaround thing because he uses a lot of freelancers. They're hungry enough not to complain too much about insane deadlines. So Irv has authorized me to supplement my existing staff with some freelancers. I came out of the meeting with a budget for that. Even though I'm going to have to back away from the overtime limits in principle, in practice some of the pressure on my staff ought to be relieved. All things considered, that's not a bad outcome."

Ironically, after Irv stated plainly that "Get it done yesterday" was the agency's policy, nearly everyone who worked there felt that the pace had become more relaxed. Steve stopped resisting last-minute assignments. The number of these requests coming from Susan declined as she became more self-assured in her dealings with clients. In her next pitch to a potential customer, she stayed in control of the meeting and landed a lucrative new account. As her confidence grew she became less agitated in her approach to the creative staff, and Rocky and Steve stopped ducking her calls. Cheri eventually decided that the time demands of the job were incompatible with her family life and resigned to freelance from home. Pronto became her principal client. Steve replaced her with a designer who was happy to work evenings and weekends in exchange for taking mornings off. Gwen relaxed and stopped trying to micromanage the creative process, much to the relief of Rocky. The *My Way* launch was a great success.

Note that none of these positive developments happened at the initiative of the CEO. The organization became less anxious because two of its middle managers decided to manage themselves. Their newfound calm rippled throughout the agency just as earlier their anxiety had done. They were able to change the system from within.

You can have a similar effect on your own workplace. If you hold a top management position, then your effects will be especially wide ranging, but even at entry level, you can make things significantly better for yourself and those in your immediate vicinity. Because you are part of a system, any positive change in yourself will provoke a positive change in others. You can become an "anxiety step down"—a point where the anxiety being passed around the system diminishes rather than escalates. The beauty of this approach is that you don't need buy-in. You don't have to propose a change and get others to agree. You can decide all by your lonesome that you want to do something about the anxiety in your organization—and then *do* it. You can start today.

Calm, collected, and clear—that's your mantra for this project. Let's talk about what it means.

Calming Yourself

The first step is to get calm. I realize that this admonishment is about as helpful as saying, "Whatever you do, don't think of a pink elephant." Being told to calm down rarely calms anyone. Nevertheless, I am telling you: get calm. Get at least approximately calm. You won't be able to think straight if your body is telling you to belt your boss, race for the nearest emergency exit, or hide under your desk. What you are trying to do here is to quiet the physiological symptoms of anxiety.

The most efficient way to get control of what's happening in your body is to focus on your breathing. It is an automatic process that you can consciously control when you want to. Breathe so deep that you feel it all the way down to your tailbone. Imagine you are sending the breath to whatever part of your body feels tense or agitated. When your breath is slow, deep, and even, it sends a message to the rest of your body. Your endocrine system gets the message, "We're being calm now." In a pinch, you can get the job done in six seconds. (See page 36.)

Getting calm also means settling down your mind, giving less energy to the thoughts that have been churning in your brain as your pulse races and your stomach ties itself in knots. You know the ones I mean. Here are some examples of unproductive thoughts:

▶ Thoughts about who's right and who's wrong

▶ Self-blame and blame of others

▶ Thoughts about who's on your side and who's against you

▶ Thoughts about how someone else ought to change

▶ Fantasies about what others are thinking or feeling about you

▶ Fantasies about what will happen next

▶ Longings for harmony and better communication.

These are really emotions pretending to be thoughts. They are expressions of anxiety. They don't tell you anything useful about the situation.

Collecting Yourself

Getting collected means thinking objectively and analytically about the emotional system you're a part of. The anxiety you are feeling is linked to the anxiety of those around you. If you are anxious, then others are anxious too. You are catching it from someone, and you are passing it on to someone else. If you are anxious, then you are both cause and effect. Usually it is easier for a person to see where their anxiety is coming from than where it is going. You will need to see both if you are to have a positive effect on the system. Here are some steps you might take in analyzing the situation:

1. *Make a map of it.* Draw a circle that represents you and other circles labeled with the names of those around you. Use arrows to indicate where anxiety is coming from and where it is going. Who were you interacting with when you became anxious? What was that person anxious about? From whom did he catch it? To whom did you pass on your anxiety, and how? What did he do with it? Your map may include people who are not part of the organization. If the demands of a family member are contributing to your anxiety at work, then put that person on the map.

Likewise include anyone outside of work who is affected by your work-related anxiety. The relationship you had to a parent when you were a child may also be part of the picture, as both Steve and Susan discovered. A person need not be physically present to be part of your anxiety map.

2. *Look for and diagram the triangles in your anxiety map.* If you are in a conflict with someone, who or what is the third point in the triangle? Who are the insiders in each triangle? Who is the outsider? If the outsider moves to an inside position, which of the present insiders is likely to be pushed to the outside? For the various triangles of which you're a part, note which individuals you are currently relating to and which you are distancing from or cutting off.

3. *Look at pursuit and distancing.* Whom are you pursuing? Who is pursuing you? From whom are you attempting to distance? Who is attempting to distance from you? In what situations are you feeling togetherness pressure? Are you, yourself, wishing for more togetherness, or are you wishing to pull away? What thoughts and impulses are you suppressing in order to maintain group harmony?

4. *Look, too, at one-up-ness and one-down-ness.* In what relationships are you taking a one-up position? In what relationships are you one-down? If you think someone is underfunctioning, where's the overfunctioner? Is it you? If you think someone is overfunctioning, what are you doing to perpetuate that?

5. *Subtract the personalities from any conflict you're a part of and identify the underlying issue.* If you are having what feels like a power struggle, then it is likely that you and your opponent are both struggling with a lack of clarity in the organization about roles, objectives, or policies. What is the decision that isn't being made?

The idea is to regard the system as dispassionately as if it were a puzzle you were trying to solve. When you take this attitude—not lamenting or moralizing about the situation—you may find yourself becoming simply *interested*. Human systems are fascinating, and as you allow yourself to become fascinated, you will discover that you're taking the situation a lot less personally.

The final step in getting collected is to take responsibility for what you are doing to perpetuate your own and others' anxiety. By this, I definitely do *not* mean taking on blame, guilt, or self-reproach. To take responsibility means to acknowledge your own power. It is a recognition that you have been affecting the system all along and can therefore affect it in a more positive direction.

When we are in anxious circumstances, it is quite natural to focus on what is beyond our control—i.e., on what other people are doing. Our anxiety is based not only on the fact that we don't like what they are doing but also on the lack of control we have over it. So we imagine that the remedy for our anxiety is to somehow *get* control. We think about what's wrong with the other person and how we can get her to change. We think the word "should" a lot. We have real or imaginary dialogues with third parties to whom we make the case that so-and-so should do such-and-such. Sometimes we imagine the solution is better communication. If the other person just understood us better, then she would stop doing the obnoxious thing she is doing. In other words, the desire for communication can be a desire to control or change someone else.

As you have already learned from experience, it doesn't work. People never do what you want them to do when you're trying to make them do what you want them to do. As long as you are trying to change the way you feel by changing what someone else is doing, you are powerless. You are the one person in an anxious situation that you *can* control. When you see that, you begin to see all sorts of options you had previously overlooked.

Being Clear

Getting clear means acting in a way that brings calm and clarity to the system you are a part of. In the course of getting collected, you will have discovered that your own anxious reactions are passing anxiety to others, contributing to the overall anxiety of the system. Once you identify the types of reactivity you are engaging in (overfunctioning, underfunctioning, pursuit, distance, triangling, blaming, scapegoating, or cutoff) you can make a conscious decision to stop reacting that way. But what do you do instead?

Each style of reactivity shares the same essential problem: you are fusing with a group or an individual. By "fusing" I mean that how you feel and what you do depends on how you think others feel and what they are doing. The solution to this problem—no matter what style of reactivity is arising from it—is to differentiate yourself from the emotional system. You are differentiating when you are able to shift your thinking away from personalities and emotions, identify the decision that is yours to make, and make it. When you are differentiated from the system, you are able to act on your own behalf without being selfish and on behalf of the group without being selfless. One expression of the differentiated self is the I-position.

To take an I-position is to let others know what you think, believe, or intend. It is based on your best thinking about the problem or issue at hand. It expresses a healthy balance between your needs and those of the organization as a whole. An I-position does not depend on what anyone else is thinking, feeling, or doing. It is what you believe to be true and valid regardless of whether or not anyone else agrees with you.

Taking an I-position stops the cycle of reactivity and brings calm to the entire system you are a part of. Often the effect is immediate, particularly if ambiguity about where you really stand is contributing to others' anxiety. For example, a major source of conflict in the Pronto Agency was uncertainty about who had the authority to establish job deadlines. When Irv finally took an I-position, stating clearly where he stood on that issue, everyone else calmed down. Even Steve, who would have preferred a different policy, was relieved to have matters clarified.

Sometimes taking an I-position temporarily raises the anxiety level, leading to pushback. You saw that happen with Steve's original I-position. It gave firm outline to a conflict that already existed between his department and the needs of the account executives and left Irv caught in the middle. But as Steve continued to maintain his position in the face of his co-workers' reactivity, they eventually came to state I-positions of their own. When that happened, the underlying issue that was making everyone anxious was clarified and resolved.

Taking an I-position doesn't mean being unwilling to compromise or cooperate with others. Steve eventually deferred to the company objectives set by Irv and cooperated fully in meeting them. The important point here is that he deferred to a *principle*, not to the reactivity of the people around him. He held firm in the face of Susan's triangling, the client's tantrums, and the togetherness pressures imposed by Irv. When he finally allowed his mind to be changed, it was by the facts, not by personalities. When Irv presented him with a new fact, he responded with a new I-position. ("If fast service is our market position, then my operation has to support that.") Coming from that new I-position, he was able to win concessions that met the needs of both his department and the agency as a whole.

While Steve and Irv set policies, not every I-position is a policy statement. Susan was taking an I-position when she told Irv that she needed clarification on the role of account executives. She did not have a position on what that role ought to be. She just needed to know what it actually was. She was also taking an I-position when she defended the design she was presenting instead of automatically accepting Gwen's changes. Cheri was taking an I-position when she decided that her working hours were incompatible with her family responsibilities. Rocky was taking an I-position when he stated that the navigation scheme proposed by Gwen wasn't going to work. Gerard was taking an I-position when he admitted that his staff couldn't sell subscriptions to a vanishing audience base. In each of these cases, the I-position consisted of forthrightly stating the facts without trying to manipulate the responses of others.

Does taking an I-position simply mean being assertive? Not exactly. Statements beginning "I want" or "I won't" are assertive, but they are not always I-positions. "I want us all to pull together as a team" is an assertive way of expressing a longing for togetherness. "I'm counting on you to support my side" is an assertive way of triangling. Taking over a meeting that someone else is supposed to be chairing is an assertive way of overfunctioning. "I want us to communicate better" is an assertive style of pursuit. "I won't work with so-and-so" is an assertive cutoff. However firmly and straightforwardly expressed, these are all anxiety reactions.

An I-position is not about what you want someone else to do or how you feel about what he or she is already doing. It's not about someone else at all. I-positions are about facts and issues, not feelings and personalities. They state what you know, believe, or intend to do about the facts and issues at hand without trying to control in any way the responses of others.

As you have seen from the examples in this book, and no doubt experienced in your own life, people become especially anxious when they are in what they see as a no-win situation. Lack of clarity about roles, policies, objectives, and overall direction leads to conflicts, power struggles, and contradictory directives. You may feel yourself caught between mutually exclusive demands, unable to please everybody. In such damned-if-you-do, damned-if-you-don't situations, most people are tempted to duck and cover, hoping to avoid blame by avoiding decision. It's a very stressful predicament to be in. If you're waiting for those around you to extricate you from it by getting their own heads straight—well, you'll probably still be waiting a year from now. The great thing about learning to take I-positions is that you can extricate yourself on your own. You take it as a given that you can't please everyone and instead take the stand that *you* believe in. Decision-making gets a lot easier when you give up the anxiety-driven belief that it's up to you to keep everyone else happy.

You Can Change the System Without Changing Other People

At this point, I'm often asked, "But what if I change my behavior and others don't changes theirs?" If you're tempted to ask this, it means that deep down you're still wishing to control other people. That's natural, for if you recognize that anxiety is systemic, you see that the anxiety reactions of others are likely to go on provoking your own anxiety. It would be nice if you could get them to stop.

You can't make anyone change by trying to make him or her change. Wanting to is an expression of anxiety and will only make others more anxious. But if you manage your own anxiety without trying to manage others', then it is inevitable that the system will change. It can't go on being exactly the way it's been unless you go on doing exactly what you're used to doing. What others will do in response to a change in you is something you can't predict and control. But, for sure, they will eventually do something different if you do something different. In the long run, that difference is likely to be better for you and the organization as a whole.

To remain calm, collected, and clear in the midst of collective anxiety is to be a leader. Regardless of your place on the organization chart, if you learn to manage yourself well when anxious, then you will have a calming effect on the system. When any individual in the reactivity chain stops being reactive, the chain is broken. Others have a chance to stop, think, and change their behavior. A person who has this effect is recognized by others as a leader, even if he is making no attempt at all to get others to follow.

When you come right down to it, we're talking about courage.

The courage to see things differently.

Anxious organizations place tremendous pressure on their members to buy-in to groupthink, to suppress "traitor thoughts" in favor of group harmony. It takes nerve to redefine problems and question quick-fix solutions.

The courage to take a stand.

A leader is clear about what he or she sees, thinks, or believes without attempting to coerce or manipulate others.

The courage to persist in the face of resistance.

When you see things differently and take a stand, the system pushes back. Pressure intensifies to return to normal, even when "normal" means chronically and miserably anxious. Chronic anxiety rarely gets better unless someone has the courage to provoke and weather a period of acute anxiety.

The courage to contain your own anxiety.

Reactions such as overfunctioning, underfunctioning, triangling, blaming, pursuit, distancing, and cutoff are strategies for getting rid of the hot potato of anxiety by handing it off to someone else. A leader pockets the hot potato instead of passing it along the chain. This requires the courage to acknowledge and endure your own anxiety.

The courage to stay in relationship with highly reactive people.

As you learn to manage your own anxiety, it is natural to wish that others would manage their own. The reactivity of others presents you with constant temptations to become reactive yourself. A leader remains calm in the face of other peoples' anxious acting out and continues to communicate.

The courage to take responsibility for yourself.

To assume leadership is to cease to blame others for your own anxiety, even when you can see that their behaviors contribute to it. Leaders focus instead on their own contribution to the problem and change the only thing that is in their power to change—themselves.

In the next chapter, I'm going to tell you the story of a leader who showed tremendous courage. Having become the focal point for the intense anxiety of a large and complex organization, he was well on his way to becoming its scapegoat—if he didn't die of a heart attack first. After learning to manage his own anxiety and modifying his behavior in a few subtle but important ways, he was able to avert a strike, save his company six million dollars, and earn a major promotion. I believe you will find his story inspiring. If he can do it, then so can you.

In Summary...

 Because anxiety is systemic, any individual within the system can change it by changing his or her own behavior. You can have a widespread positive effect on your organization by learning to remain calm, collected, and clear in the face of systemic anxiety.

 The first step is to calm your physiological reactions to anxiety and identify the repetitive and unproductive thoughts that accompany it.

 Become collected by analyzing how anxiety travels throughout the system and your own role as an anxiety carrier. Look objectively at the patterns (overfunctioning, underfunctioning, pursuit, distancing, cutoff, blame, triangling, and conflict) you and others fall into when you are anxious.

 Become clear by differentiating yourself from the emotional system. This means dropping your reactive patterns and taking I-positions instead.

 An I-position is a forthright statement of what you know, believe, or intend to do. It is based on facts and issues, not feelings and personalities.

 An I-position will, in some cases, have an immediate calming effect on the system. In other cases, it may temporarily raise anxiety to an acute level. If you have the courage to remain firm during this acute phase, then underlying issues can be addressed and systemic anxiety will, in the long run, diminish.

▶▶Chapter 8

The Power of One

Changing the system from within

This is the story of a real-life hero. Only the identifying details have been changed, to protect client confidentiality.

Its setting is Beanie Bros. Coffee, one of the nation's oldest packagers of coffee and tea. Over the years Beanie Bros. had bought up many smaller companies, using some of their plants to package products sold under the Beanie Bros. label and allowing others to go on producing regional brands. At the time our story begins, the company had just been reorganized and a new president, named. As part of the reorganization effort, regional plants that had previously operated with a lot of independence were being converted to the Beanie Bros. management model.

For most of the company's history, coffee and tea had been sold as commodities with little to distinguish one brand from another except name recognition and price. With the advent of franchise cafés and the growing consumer preference for premium coffees during the 1990s, the company was faced with the need to shift its emphasis to marketing. Internally, this meant that marketing executives were developing newfound clout while production executives felt their own power to be diminishing. The new competitors were also chipping away at the company's profitability, which had traditionally been robust. Many of the top executives were nearing retirement and heavily vested in Beanie Bros. stock. All of these factors contributed to the organization's overall anxiety.

The original Beanie Bros. plant was located in New Jersey. All of the company's top executives had served there at some point in their careers. Because of their familiarity with it, the plant tended to receive a lot of management scrutiny. It was also a source of worry. The union environment was particularly strong in this plant. At the time our story begins, the union contract was about to expire, and the company was bracing itself for a protracted strike. Our hero, Herb, had the thankless job of managing this plant.

As an executive, Herb was on the slow track, having been promoted to plant manager rather late in his career. Though technically quite capable, he was prone to losing his temper and antagonizing subordinates. Management had misgivings about putting him in charge of the volatile New Jersey plant, and as labor tensions mounted there, Herb had begun to justify these misgivings. As one of his subordinates described it, Herb seemed "to go from lamb to lion and back again overnight." He had alienated the supervisors to such an extent that they were beginning to side with the union, despite being on the management team themselves. Essentially, the union had taken over the plant, which seemed to be producing more grievances than coffee.

Herb was also caught between Rachel, the VP for marketing, and Stan, the regional director of operations, to whom Herb officially reported. In principle, there was no reason for a plant manager to be taking orders from a marketing director. But Rachel's marketing initiatives involved the redesign of packaging, which gave her occasion to stick her nose into production. She also enjoyed enormous unofficial power due to the fact that she had the company's biggest customer in her pocket. The personal dislike Stan and Rachel felt for one another was exacerbated by a lack of clarity at the top of the organization about their respective roles. Rachel was constantly calling Herb to give him advice or orders and then instructing him not to tell Stan. Herb, caught in the middle, was trying to please them both by following mutually exclusive directives.

Herb had come to the verge of resigning several times, only to change his mind. The company wanted to retain him yet worried that if he didn't quit, he might die of a heart attack. During his tenure as plant manager, he had gained nearly sixty pounds. The weight gain, combined with his emotional volatility and evident stress, caused general concern for his health. Realizing that he could use some help, the director of executive development called me and asked me to coach Herb on managing people—and his own stress—a little better.

First Meeting—October 14

The first time I visited his office, I found Herb as frazzled as I'd been led to expect. Face flushed and tie askew, he was poring over a pile of union grievances on a desk speckled with donut crumbs.

Most of the grievances concerned overtime. Some workers grieved because they had been assigned overtime that they didn't want. Others grieved because they hadn't been assigned overtime that they did want. "The union wants to run the place," he said. "And they're succeeding. They've got me so buried in all these penny-ante disputes, I don't have time for much else."

Herb's attempted solution to the problem was to take work schedules into his own hands, assigning overtime according to the expressed wishes of the workers rather than the provisions of the union contract. It wasn't helping. The wishes of the individual workers seemed to change arbitrarily from day to day. The more he tried to accommodate them, the more they felt entitled to be indignant if their scheduling preferences were not met. To make matters worse, in taking over the schedule, Herb was usurping the role of the plant foremen. Confronted with the complaints of their workers, the foremen would throw up their hands and say, "Don't talk to me about it. I have no control. Herb calls all the shots around here."

"What the hell am I supposed to do?" Herb said, his voice rising to a shout. "I try to be the manager they want. But what in blazes do they want? Would someone please tell me that?" He bit savagely into another donut. "Meanwhile, I've got Rachel on my case about retooling the baggers to make these confounded yuppified packages the designers come up with. Naturally they know zip about how baggers actually work. Like you can just go from plastic to heat-stamped foil overnight. Stan tells me to get the machinists doing one thing, and then Rachel comes along and tells them to do something else, only don't tell Stan. And then I'm supposed to somehow explain to Stan why the machinists aren't doing it his way. As if I have any control."

He eyed the half-eaten donut sitting on his pile of grievances with amused distain. "Honey-glazed Prozac," he remarked. "That's what I usually do about stress. Would you believe when I started this job, I had a thirty-six-inch waist? Now look at the gut on me."

This seemed as good an opening as any to teach Herb some stress-reduction techniques. I led him on a guided relaxation exercise and then taught him how to take a six-second vacation. "Whew!" he said, when he opened his eyes again. "That sure feels better."

Once Herb was calm, I explained to him how anxiety moves through systems and helped him analyze some of the elements of his situation in systems terms. You, the reader, may already have recognized in it some of the anxiety-containment patterns discussed earlier in this book.

▶ Herb, in taking over the schedule, as well as nearly every other decision made in the plant, had been overfunctioning. This had led, predictably, to underfunctioning on the part of the foremen.

▶ Each time a worker didn't like one of Herb's decisions, the foremen found it expedient to side with the worker against Herb. In other words, triangles kept springing up in which Herb was put in the outsider position.

▶ Grievances triggered further triangles in which Herb, once again, held the outside position.

▶ In the Herb-Rachel-Stan triangle, Herb occupied the inside position. Because Rachel and Stan were in extreme conflict, this inside position was very uncomfortable. Each time he tried to please one, he antagonized the other.

▶ Overtime had become a heated issue not because it was being abused to any great extent by management but because open conflict over the issue was serving as an outlet for anxiety in the plant as a whole.

▶ Much of this anxiety could be traced to ambiguity about where Herb stood as leader. His first reaction to anxiety was to want to please whoever was demanding or complaining at any given moment. Since demands being made on him were contradictory, what he would do next was unpredictable. There were no coherent principles underlying his decisions. Periodically he would become exasperated by his inability to please everybody and blow up at the nearest person, thereby feeding more anxiety into the system.

▶ When the stress got to be too much for Herb—
which was usually, these days—he would shut
himself up in his office, distancing almost to
the point of cutoff. This increased the feeling of
ambiguity about him, and everyone else's anxiety.

The patterns of anxiety containment in the plant
mirrored Herb's own. In other words, Herb was highly
reactive, so everyone else was too. It is rare that the emotional maturity of a group exceeds that of its leader. That's
the bad news. The good news, as I went on to explain to
Herb, is that any positive change in the leader will have a
marked and widespread impact on the organization as a
whole. To get a handle on the plant, Herb needed first to
get a handle on himself.

Second Meeting—October 24

Ten days later, I found Herb ebullient.
"Objectively, not much has changed," he admitted. "Since I last saw you, I've been served with
ten more grievances. Ten! We've crossed the line
into complete absurdity. But still, I'm feeling better. I'm seeing there's a light at the end of this tunnel. It's a long way off,
but it's there."

He continued, "I'm out on the plant floor more. Make it a practice to go out and just walk around at least twice each day. That was hard at first, but it seems to be making a difference. People seem more willing to talk to me. And you know what? I can see what you were talking about last time. When I'm anxious, the plant is anxious. I can actually see that for myself. It's amazing. Oh, and I've been taking six-second vacations right and left!" he concluded with a laugh.

I asked him how he was handling the grievance epidemic.

"Stan gave me a great idea about that. He suggested that I delay responding for seven days. Look," he said, sliding open the top drawer of his desk to reveal a pile of unopened envelopes. "I just drop them in here. Don't even look at them until seven days have passed. Might seem like a small thing, but I think it's going to make a difference. The union isn't pulling my strings anymore. They can't get me to drop whatever I'm doing the moment someone files a complaint. At any rate, letting the things cool off for a while sure makes me feel calmer. And that's bound to help, right?"

Herb was on the high that often accompanies the first breakthrough into systems thinking. He had discovered the power of his anxiety to make those around him anxious and, conversely, the power to change the system by calming down. He was beginning to differentiate himself from the emotional force field with which he had earlier been fused. He was seeing that he didn't have to allow it to control him. His celebratory mood was well deserved. Every subsequent positive change was to spring from this first big insight.

Third Meeting—December 5

When we next met, six weeks later, Herb's whole demeanor sagged. He seemed both worried and weary. His remarks were full of self-reproach.

"I got caught between the union and the foremen at a grievance meeting yesterday," he began. "Forgot everything you told me about triangling and all. If I had an I-position, well—" he laughs ruefully, "my position was just that I wanted the whole thing to go away. That's all I was thinking about. I didn't have a clue where I really stood, so how was anyone else to know? I just let myself get jerked up, down, and sideways by both sides. It was a fiasco."

"Noticing this systems stuff isn't always so great," he continued. "I'm starting to see a lot of things that I wish I didn't see. Like how my family is a system too, and how it's connected to this one here at the plant. Through me, I mean. I take my stress home, and there I cut myself off just like I used to do in the office. Zone out in front of the tube with a bag of chips and might as well be deaf for all I hear of what Alice and the kids are saying to me. Not that they're saying much these days. I think they gave up on me about forty pounds ago. I'm shut up in all this fat like it's some door I'm closing."

He pauses to crack open the seal on a bottle of mineral water. "Trying to do something about that, at least" he explains. "No more honey-glazed Prozac."

"So you're feeling your anxiety more. Because what you used to do to get rid of it, you're no longer doing."

"Right. And to tell you the truth, it sucks. All this awareness. I know I'm supposed to be the leader of this system, but I have trouble feeling my own power as leader. I have trouble acknowledging that. Mostly I feel like it has power over me. For instance, try as I might, I can't get anyone to be straight with me. The foremen just tell me what I want to hear. I don't know why we bother to talk at all. Nothing real gets said. They just nod to my face and then go off and do heaven knows what."

"How about you?" I asked. "What do you tell them?"

"Ah, got me there. I'm the same way. Tell people what they want to hear. Kind of set the pattern for the organization, I guess."

"That's still happening?"

"I hate to admit it but, yes. I'll give you an example. I'm doing my walking-around thing, and a guy on the line starts bending my ear about this whole big worker-empowerment scheme he's into. Real smart guy he is, and he's been doing all this reading about getting rid of fixed job categories and making every production decision as a group. And there I am nodding and grinning my encouragement, and on one level, I'm really into what he's saying. I think it's a pretty interesting idea. So I tell him maybe we can try something like that. Next thing I know, Rachel's on the phone blistering my ear about delivery backlogs, wanting me to crack the whip. I get off that call, phone rings right away again, and this time it's Stan, telling me I've got to ease up on people; the union's bitching about the pressure I'm putting on them to package a little coffee when they can take a break from manufacturing grievances...!"

He paused to take a deep breath. "Sorry, I'm ranting. The point is, I think back on what that guy on the line was saying, and I realize there's no way. No way we're going to implement a scheme like that in this environment. I've all I can do to get people to do their own jobs without 'empowering' them to do someone else's. So why did I lead him on like that? It wasn't honest. It was just me going whatever way the wind blows."

Herb would have been surprised to hear that I thought he was doing fine. The negativity he was feeling was actually a sign that he was becoming more differentiated from the anxiety in the system. Where previously he had acted unconsciously, now he was able to step back and watch himself react. This new self-consciousness was not pleasant since he wasn't liking what he saw. Nevertheless, it was a positive development. It would eventually enable him to catch himself in the act of sliding into old patterns and reverse himself on the spot.

Another reason Herb was discouraged was that the system was pushing back. Triangles, in particular, can be quite tenacious, and Herb was embroiled in a lot of triangles. It was going to take persistence to break up the embedded triangles he had gotten into around union issues, and he would have to step very carefully to extricate himself from the triangle with Rachel and Stan.

Fourth Meeting—December 23

Three weeks later, I noticed that Herb looked markedly thinner. "I've lost almost twenty pounds this past month," he confirmed. "When I realize I'm feeling anxious, I take a six-second vacation instead of feeding my face. I'm not even tempted to bury my anxiety that way anymore. I look back now and realize how miserable that was making me."

Despite the discouragement he had confided at the previous session, Herb had persisted in changing his own behavior, and now he was beginning to see positive results in the plant. He had been concentrating especially on his tendency to overfunction. He informed the foremen that he would no longer involve himself in scheduling and that overtime was to be assigned in compliance with the union contract rather than the whims of individual workers. "It's amazing how quickly that worked," Herb remarked. "Like the moment I stopped interfering, they started to do their jobs. If workers come to me with a complaint, I tell them to take it up with their own supervisor. I was worried that the foremen wouldn't be firm enough, for there's been this tendency for them to side with the union against the plant. But now that I'm treating them like managers, they're acting like managers."

Herb's perception was that the anxiety level within the plant had dropped considerably. One objective sign of this was that, since our last meeting, only two grievances had been filed. Both were killed by the union. Stan had noticed the change in atmosphere and complimented Herb on how well things were going. Rachel, too, had remarked that Herb seemed to be in better control of the plant. "It's the only thing those two have ever agreed on!" he laughed.

"Remember that guy on the line I told you about, the one with the empowerment scheme? I was kind of tempted to avoid him after that. But instead I went up to him last week and gave him a straight answer. I told him that the change he was proposing was not in the cards, that it just doesn't fit with the Beanie Bros. management model. I also said that I saw leadership ability in him that probably wasn't going to find an outlet in his current position and that I'd be misleading him if I said the job description was ever going to change. A few days later he comes back and tells me he's applying to business school. Asked me to write him a letter of recommendation, which I was happy to do. He told me it meant a lot to him that I hadn't just blown him off."

Fifth Meeting—January 17

Things were still going well when Herb and I met three weeks later. "Remember how I said that the foremen just tell me what I want to hear? It's different now. I'm noticing that as I get straighter about where I stand on issues, they're getting straighter too. Not just with me but also with the workers.

"The head machinist has even gotten straight with Rachel," he continued. "Gave her a lesson on how retooling works, what was and wasn't feasible in terms of packaging design. It came as news to her because always before he'd just nod and say okay when she presented him with an unworkable design, and then I'd catch hell later when he wasn't able to execute it. So she comes to me and says we need a new bagger, which I happen to agree with. But that's really Stan's call, so I told her to make her proposal to him. Then Stan calls me, all upset that Rachel's sticking her nose into operations again and peeved that I was encouraging her. So I said to him, just as I'd said to Rachel, that capital equipment is his call and that, in my judgment, the bagger is nearing the end of its useful life and should probably be upgraded sooner rather than later."

"How did that go over?" I asked.

"Great. He's in negotiations with the manufacturer now, and, at my suggestion, Rachel is participating. If they want to hate each other, that's their business, but since package design depends on the capabilities of the equipment, it seems reasonable that the VP of Marketing should have input."

"So you were motivated by practical considerations rather than the personal clash between Rachel and Stan."

"Exactly. I got myself out of the middle on that one. And the funny thing is, they both seem to trust me more. I get the feeling everyone trusts me more these days. That puzzles me. Seems to me I've been trustworthy all along."

If you view trust as a moral or ethical issue, Herb is right—he had never been less than ethical and fair in his dealings with others. Lack of trust seldom has much to do with the moral character of the person who isn't trusted. It is an expression of anxiety. There is uncertainty in the system as a whole. When objectives, policies, or roles are poorly defined or inconsistently enforced, then members of the organization focus excessively on the personality of the leader. They imagine that what will happen depends on the leader's moods and whims. When such matters are treated objectively, with clarity and consistency, everyone calms down. The leader's personality hasn't changed, but it no longer arouses anxiety because people understand that what will happen does not depend on that personality.

Our work together was essentially finished by the end of this session. Herb had learned to manage his own anxiety, and as a result the plant as a whole was calming down. The change in him was so marked that people had begun to ask what had come over him. He used these exchanges as opportunities to teach others how to take a six-second vacation. "Now everybody's taking them," he chuckled. "In the middle of a tense meeting, you'll suddenly hear someone take a big deep breath, and everyone else will laugh and say, 'Here comes another six-second vacation!' I've started a trend."

By now, Herb was able to think pretty consistently in systems terms. He'd gotten his tendency to overfunction under control and was beginning to extricate himself from persistent triangles. He was becoming confident that when new anxiety patterns arose in himself or others, he could understand what was going on and act appropriately. "I'm able to see my own anxiety now in the moment when it's happening. I'm able to stop myself on the spot when I'm about to slide into an old pattern."

Followup—April 2

When Herb called me in early spring, it was the first time we'd spoken in nearly four months. He had a lot of news to share, and all of it was good.

"You know that strike we were all expecting?" he began. "It didn't happen. The company had been thinking it was inevitable. They'd already budgeted six million dollars to cover it. But it didn't happen."

I knew that the company had indeed been resigned to a strike because the director of executive development had mentioned it when she first asked me to work with Herb. She had told me that the company didn't consider Herb responsible for the union situation and did not expect that improving his performance as a manager would avert a strike. It had not been an objective of our work together, so I was as surprised as anyone to learn that the strike had been averted after all.

"How'd you manage it?" I asked.

"Well, the whole management team handled themselves really well during the negotiations. Our strategy was to set up informal meetings with the union before the official negotiating sessions began. We laid out exactly what we wanted, and why, and what we were willing to offer. So the union knew exactly what they could expect from us, going in. No surprises. No head games. I think another factor in the situation was that over the past few months, all these joint management/union teams have been springing up to address specific problems. That wasn't my doing—I mean, I wasn't directly trying to organize anything like that. It just started to happen as the foremen got more on the ball—"

"You mean when you stopped overfunctioning?" I put in.

"Exactly. They started taking more responsibility, and it seems like everyone got more willing to communicate, and the result was they started forming these ad hoc task forces. So by the time we got to the contract talks, relations with the union had become a lot less adversarial. Instead of constantly grieving about overtime, they began to give more thought to what they wanted the policy to be, overall. They came to the bargaining table with a pretty good proposal. The talks wrapped up a month early, and both sides came away feeling satisfied with the new contract. Neither side had to make a big sacrifice."

Herb had more good news. Over the past quarter, plant productivity had gone up 30 percent and errors had declined by a similar factor. "That's partly due to the work of the task forces," he said. "But it may also be due to the fact that people have started putting energy into production that used to go into conflicts. So we're looking real good around here."

On a more personal level, Herb was also doing great. He had by now dropped forty-seven pounds and reported that he and his family had begun to communicate. "Alice told me the other day that I've turned back into the man she married. She seems happier these days."

"What I still can't get over is how simple it was," Herb said. "I won't say easy. But simple. I just made a few small changes in what I was doing, and everyone around me started to change. I wasn't even trying to change them. I just got my own act together, and, like magic, the whole plant starts getting its act together."

A month later, Herb was offered a promotion. Beanie Bros. had acquired a new plant, and Herb was to oversee the transition. In six months, he had transformed himself from the plant manager everyone believed was hanging on by a thread into something of legend: the guy who turned around the troubled New Jersey plant.

In conclusion, I can't improve on Herb's own words. Turning around an anxious organization isn't easy. But it is simple. An individual who shows courage in the face of his or her own anxiety can transform a herd of stampeding wildebeests into a sane, smart, and effective organization.

Additional Reading

Bowen Center for the Study of the Family.
    www.georgetownfamilycenter.org
Bowen, M., Kerr. 1988. *Family Evaluation* New York: W.W. Norton &
    Company, Inc.
Comella, P., J. Bader, J. Ball, K. Wiseman, and R. Sagar. 1995. *The
    Emotional Side of Organizations*. Washington, DC: Georgetown Family
    Center
Damasio, A. 1994. *Descartes' Error*. New York: Avon Books.
Friedman, E. 1985. *Generation to Generation*. New York: Guilford Press.
Gilbert, R. 1992. *Extraordinary Relationships*. Minneapolis: Chronimed
    Publishing.
Goleman, D. 1995. *Emotional Intelligence*. New York: Bantam Books.
Lerner, H. 1985. *The Dance of Anger*. New York: Harper & Row
    Publishers, Inc.
Papero, D. 1997. *Bowen Family Systems Theory*. Boston: Allyn & Bacon.
Riley, R., and K. Wiseman. 1982. *Understanding Organizations*.
    Washington, DC: Georgetown Family Center.
Sapolsky, R. 1998. *Why Zebras Don't Get Ulcers*. New York: W.H.
    Freeman.

About The Author:

Jeffrey A. Miller, MSW, has worked with countless anxious organizations during his career—and has also seen many of them come up with brilliant and unexpected solutions to their problems. His myriad experiences have given him a unique perspective on creating healthy workplaces. Through his company, Jeffrey Miller + Associates, he helps businesses attain key goals and objectives by increasing their organizational effectiveness. He has experience as a family therapist, organizational consultant and coach to top executives in corporate and not-for-profit settings.

For over 20 years, clients across a wide range of industries and business functions have called on Miller's support and guidance in such areas as developing effective leadership, managing crises, improving performance/productivity, designing and structuring organizations, assessing/changing corporate cultures, building successful teams, and managing the demands of transition.

If you would like more information, please contact Jeffrey Miller + Associates, 1100 N. East Avenue, Oak Park, IL 60302, (866) 509-0500 (toll-free), or visit www.anxiousorg.com. You may also contact Jeffrey A. Miller by e-mail at jmiller@anxiousorg.com.

Index

C

Calming down, 33-35, 56-57, 159, 166, 173-175, 179, 183, 197, 204
Canary in the mineshaft, 147-151
Cerebral cortex, 33
Changing behavior, vii-viii, 26, 29, 138-140, 183-187, 201
Cheetahs, 9
Children, 97, 176
Chronic anxiety, 54, 57, 85, 112, 144, 148, 150, 161, 185
Circus performers, 60
Clarity, 159-161, 178-182, 192
    lack of, 158, 177, 182
Client factors, v
Client satisfaction, 169
Cliques, 16
Coalitions, 16
Cockroaches, 4
Coffee break, 34
Collecting yourself, 175-178
Collective anxiety reaction, 64
Common adversary. See Shared adversary.
Communication, 157-158, 174, 181, 206
    gap, 103
    lack of, 17
Competition, 9
Confidence, 119
Conflict, 159, 161, 187
    as natural, 142
    as not personal, 157
    avoidance of, 54, 142
    between two people, 105-106, 110, 114
    getting to root of, 151-157
    healthy, 142
    mismanaged, 143
    needs in, 157
    perception of, 161
Conflicting demands, 54
Conflicting instructions, 17
Conformity. See Consensus.

Consensus, 74-79. 88
    appearance of, 78
    as time consuming, 78
Consequences, 44
Constantly seeking advice, 131, 140
Control, 14, 80, 130, 145, 177
    loss of, 136
    of feelings, 137
    of reactions, 56-57
    of the behavior of others, 41-42, 77, 177-178
Coping mechanisms, 38
Corpse. See Human body.
Courage, 85, 184-186, 208
Co-workers, 6, 14
Criminal conspiracy, 98
Customer demands, 9
Cutting off, 176, 178, 182, 185, 187, 196
Cycles of anxiety, 17, 26, 28
Cyclone fence, 108

D

Danger. See Threat.
Daydreaming, 68-74
Dead-wood employees. See Employees.
Debate, 79, 158
Decisions, 130-131, 140
Degree of contact, 72
Delegating authority, 136
Demands
    illegitimate vs. legitimate, 106
    mutually exclusive, 182
Departments, 133
Differentiating. See Emotional system.
Discomfort, vi, 102
Displacement of fight/flight/freeze response, 33
Displeasure, 42, 54, 90, 138
Distancer, 70, 87
Distancing, 17, 35-36, 69-75, 79, 87, 97, 130, 146, 148, 162, 176, 178, 185, 187, 195
Doing an end run, 102
Dominant ape, 17

H

I

J

K

U

V

W